Alan Jones

Students!

Do Not Push Your Teacher Down the Stairs on Friday

A TEACHER'S NOTEBOOK

QUADRANGLE BOOKS
A New York Times Company

Typography and Binding Design by Joan Stoliar

FOR LINDA

.

Contents

I should like to thank Nick Micelli, Harold Goldblatt, John Miller, Marshall Gold, William Walker, and George Tye for their friendship during my stay at Du Sable. It was the only thing that kept me teaching through those long, cold Chicago winters. Most of all I thank my wife, Linda, whose constant encouragement and criticism made this book possible.

A.J.

Chicago 1972

What follows is a true account—the events and the people are real. I have changed names and their connection with particular events for obvious reasons.

1. "This Place is a Jungle!"

*M*y first day at Du Sable Upper Grade Center was an exciting one. It had all the characteristics that Herbert Kohl and John Herndon have well documented. The broken windows were there along with the torn window shades and broken desk tops, appendages to the badly lighted, worn central hallway. It seemed to me that first day that even the physical plant of Du Sable encouraged failure and a sense of depression.

All teachers were told to report to Room 179, which would become my division room for the coming year. After I had contorted my body to fit the small dimensions of a desk, I very carefully observed my colleagues—the people with whom I would be professionally associated during the coming year. I was struck immediately by the two distinct groups of teachers that had formed. Towards the front of the room were mostly young teachers with long hair, bell-bottoms, and paperback books in their back pockets. In the back of the room were the older teachers. While their dress was certainly not conservative, their clothes seemed cumbersome, almost too heavy for their bodies to hold up.

I listened to the younger teachers talking about such matters as Norman Mailer, Karl Marx, and Summerhill,

3

and some were even debating when and in what form the revolution would come. Their conversations were ripe with such chic phrases as "right on," "power to the people," and "let's get ourselves together." In truth, I was impressed with their apparent intellectual capabilities and their sensitivity to the situation they found themselves in. With so enlightened a faculty, we stood a good chance of rooting out the ignorance and apathy which I had read existed in the student body of such schools as Du Sable. It would be quite a battle. All the odds were against us. At least that was what that visiting teacher from the ghetto school had told me in my course on socially disadvantaged children, in which I had received an A.

What did he know?, I thought. He was a white racist who kept saying the kids needed discipline and structure. To be open and free would mean disaster, he said, maybe even physical harm. What rubbish! What the system can do to some people. No wonder the blacks are burning buildings. Education is the key. I will be the key.

I was sure that this faculty and these new kids would prove that racist a liar and in the process raise these poor kids' reading scores by three, maybe even four, years. We would beat the system at its own game. As I looked up at the room's torn bulletin boards with the inscription "Stone run it," I felt proud that I was involved in this experiment. In the words of one of my compatriots sitting next to me, "We are all about to do something beautiful."

While I was staring at the torn bulletin board, my thoughts were interrupted by talk coming from the back of the room. I turned to find one young mustachioed teacher with his head in his hands saying to the teacher sitting next to him, a chain-smoker, "Shit, I hope I don't get killed this year. One more semester and I'll have my Master's and then Simpson [the principal] can take this goddam school and shove it up his ass."

I was confused. The faculty of my dream had included the back part of the room as well. I was counting on the experienced teachers to offer leadership. Unobtrusively, I turned around to listen to the older teachers' conversation to see if this man's talk was representative or if he was just another racist.

The man next to me was black with a rather large goatee. He looked as if he had been drinking all night. I asked him if this was his first year at Du Sable, and he said no, he had been there three years. I then cautiously asked him what kind of year it was going to be.

"Well," he said, "I'm ready for the little bastards. This year I'm gonna use a steel pipe, not wood. Wood breaks too easy. Steel will stop most anybody."

Someone called him from the back of the room and he left without excusing himself. Who was this man? Did he really use physical violence in his classroom? Before I could rationalize this man's obvious betrayal of his own people, my attention along with most of the faculty's was drawn to a large, well-built black man who entered the room from the back door. Aside from his massive frame, his voice—which, raspy and cracked, sounded like Louis Armstrong's—immediately commanded the attention of most of us in the room.

The chain-smoker sitting behind me looked over his shoulder and said, "Thank God. The coach is back." The coach, whose name was Mills, moved to a seat by the window, making comments to various teachers as he

5

passed, and now and then letting out a hardy laugh in response to a friend's comment. I could catch only some of his remarks, which all seemed to have the same ending—"Yeah, I'm back to kick more black ass," invariably followed by a short laugh. With the appearance of Coach Mills the depression in the back of the room diminished, and the teachers there all began to talk about the exploits of the coach.

"Do you remember when that high school kid threatened to kill the coach?" asked the chain-smoker behind me to the man seated beside him.

"Yes, the coach looked him straight in the eyes and told the kid to name the time and the place. Then the kid like a damn fool told him he would meet him in the back of the cafeteria during the first few minutes of the lunch period. Goddammit if the coach didn't show up in the cafeteria every sixth period with his baseball bat and paddle to look for that little bastard."

"I used to eat lunch that period," said the chain-smoker, "and all you could hear in the teacher's cafeteria was Coach Mills yelling, 'Where the hell is that black bastard who was going to kill me?! All you kids are the same, full of shit. Most of you must spend your whole day wiping your ass.' " They laughed uproariously.

Standing in back of the chain-smoker was a short young man with his hair curling up on the back of his neck. He leaned over and said, "What about the time they broke into the gym and shit all over his floor. Boy, was he pissed."

"Yeah," said the chain-smoker's friend, "I was on hall patrol when he discovered it. He came charging out of those two big iron doors shouting at the top of his lungs,

'Those black bastards shit on my floor.' Then he dragged me into the gym to show me what they had done. That day he made all his gym classes pull down their pants while he personally checked assholes for evidence. He's too fuckin' much.''

I leaned over and asked the chain-smoker if the coach really checked the kids.

"You're damn right he did. What we need in this school is more people to check assholes. Let's face it, this place is a jungle. To survive you act like you're in the jungle, and the coach is probably the best goddam jungle fighter we've got.'' His friends looked on, nodding their heads in agreement.

I turned around in my desk just in time to hear the end of a debate on Bakunin's anarchism between two long-haired teachers in front of me. While listening to the end of the argument, I could not get my mind off the chain-smoker, his friends, or the black man with the goatee. They seemed so totally negative, so bitter. What had made them like that? Did every teacher in the back of the room feel as they did? Were the kids really bastards? Did the coach really check assholes? The answers to these questions would have to wait, because the principal had just walked in and was ready to begin the meeting.

"Pardon Me"

*T*he principal, a Negro of medium build who looked to be in his mid-forties, began the meeting by thanking all the teachers for being on time and wishing everyone had had a good vacation. He then asked all the new teachers to stand up and introduce themselves. I noticed that more than half the staff were brand-new.

This observation was also made by the mustachioed teacher behind me, who said to the chain-smoker, "Boy, are we going to get our asses kicked this year!" The principal was silently counting the number of teachers while the introductions were going on. After everyone sat down, he asked his vice-principal to go right downstairs and inform downtown that we were twenty teachers short. Then he looked around and began his orientation.

"Good morning, teachers, my name is Mr. Simpson, and I am the Acting Principal. Seated next to me is Mr. De Neal, the Acting Assistant Principal, and seated next to Mr. De Neal is Mr. Brand, our other Acting Assistant Principal." He then introduced the Master Teachers and some of the clerks from the office.

Simpson went on to explain where and when we could get our materials and whom to ask if we wanted filmstrips.

"Now that you are all acquainted with the facilities here at Du Sable," Simpson continued, "I would like to tell you what I expect of you and, most important, what I feel will enrich the ongoing educational program here at Du Sable. First, every teacher should keep accurate records. Each teacher will receive a record book and these will be checked periodically by downtown. Second, every teacher will be given a plan book, which must be turned in every week and checked for completeness. Third, all communications from the office should be answered immediately, no matter what is going on in your classroom. Fourth, be sure your bulletin board assignments are interesting, show classroom involvement, and are up on time. Finally, we should all be aware that we are here to educate children."

I was relieved that Simpson had finally gotten around to the educational program. Wasn't his order of priorities mixed up? Well, hell, who was I to question him?

"Are there any questions concerning your responsibilities or what you are to do today?"

The chain-smoker raised his hand and asked if the school would have any additional security this year.

"Pardon me," replied Simpson, "I was not aware of any security problem last year." (The entire back of the room grunted in unison.) The chain-smoker retorted, "Mr. Simpson, we had one teacher stabbed in the back and another one hit on the head, and numerous examples of verbal and minor physical assault in the hallways! Aren't those incidents, Mr. Simpson, enough grounds for beefing up the security personnel this year?" Simpson looked a bit annoyed at the chain-smoker, but managed to smile. "Mr. Portelli, the incidents which you have just sighted were unfortunate. But the question I ask, and we all should be asking, is why those accidents happened? Would the addition of police in the building help the situation, or could the school take more positive steps in the area of our educational program to prevent such accidents?"

I heard the coach say, "What the hell is wrong with that man? He's going to get all of us killed."

"Mr. Mills, do you have a comment?"

"No, Mr. Simpson."

Across the room an older black man stood up. He was impressive, about six foot six. He asked Simpson how discipline was going to be handled this year.

Portelli's friend leaned over and whispered, "Here comes the bullshit."

"Mr. Lincoln, I'm glad you brought that up because I feel that all these new teachers should realize that when they go into the classroom they have the office in back of them."

"What did I tell you?" whispered the chain-smoker's friend.

"I will let one of the counselors answer that question."

A big man in the front stood up and showed everyone a discipline card. "If anything happens in your class, you should fill out this card completely and tell the student you have taken this action. If the student accumulates three cards the parent should be called. If you cannot reach the parent, then send out a community representative and he will get the student's parent for you. If all these measures fail, then send the student down to the office for counseling. Be sure that no student comes down until you have followed proper procedures. But if the student has a weapon, or physically assaults you, then you should come down and fill out an accident report immediately."

The tall black teacher in the corner asked if it would be possible to cut down all the red tape in the discipline procedure and just have a room where unruly students could be sent immediately so it would be possible to conduct the class. The counselor said it would be impossible to set up a discipline room because there were not enough rooms to go round in the first place. Besides, it was the teacher's responsibility to exhaust all efforts before sending the student down.

Simpson stood up abruptly. "Pardon me. But I would like to remind all you teachers that Board policy states that you should not use corporal punishment on any student." I could hear Coach Mills laughing in the back. "We are professionals, and as professionals we should deal with discipline problems in a professional manner and not resort to any type of physical coercion." I could hear the coach trying to muffle his laughter. "If there are no further questions, all teachers should report to their rooms and put up an attractive bulletin board to welcome the students and do any necessary planning for their educational program."

Teachers in the back of the room began to move out the back door when Mr. Williams, a Master Teacher, stood up and asked all teachers to remain in the room because he had something of importance to add to Simpson's comments. The teachers came back to their seats visibly annoyed at the request, and I could hear Coach Mills say, "What the hell now?"

"Before you teachers go to your rooms be sure to pick up your record books on the table outside this room. Last year we had a great deal of trouble with teachers who did not keep accurate records. This will not be tolerated this year. Remember, the sole reason for you being here is to keep these records up to date. The rest of your duties are secondary. Do I make myself clear? Now all teachers may proceed to their respective rooms."

While the other teachers moved out I remained. This was my room, and even if it wasn't, I was a bit stunned by the last announcement. No one even raised their hand to question the statement. How can a record book take priority in a school where all the kids are reading below grade level? I realized that records were important, but were they the sole reason for being here?

When the room was empty, I began to clean up. I arranged the chairs in neat rows and straightened up my desk. In the top drawer I found a handful of truant slips which I quickly threw away, thinking I would have no need for them. After all, when I was in school I never knew anyone who was truant. I also found some discipline cards and almost threw them away—but I thought just maybe one or two kids might need a scare, and so I kept them.

My next project was the bulletin boards. I tried to think of what John Holt would put up. It had to be something special, something that would establish a learning environment. The kids needed something to reorient them to the classroom and immediately to challenge their imaginations.

After some thought I put upon my smallest board, "Welcome back to Du Sable, I'm ready to learn with you." A catchy phrase! My students and I would both go through the learning process together. What could be more rewarding? On the back board I put up pictures of famous blacks in the news and left an open section with the heading, "Can you add any?" I stepped back to look around and felt proud of myself. Even though there weren't any shades on the windows and most of the panes were broken, the boards livened up the room. I felt myself off to a good start.

I sat down at my desk and wrote out some plans for the next day. Nothing definite, just questions I was going to ask the students about their ideas on where they wanted to go this year. I refused to cram education down their throats. I would teach them what they wanted to learn. How could I have discipline problems if all the kids were happy with what they were doing? Simpson has a point, I thought. A teacher like Portelli makes them write their spelling words ten times each and do exercises in their grammar book on subjects and verbs. No wonder he sounded so bitter.

The dismissal bell rang, bringing me out of my thoughts. I collected my record book and some loose papers, walked to the door, and took a final look at the room: yes, I was going to do something beautiful this year.

3. First Day.

I arrived at Du Sable early the next morning, not because I had anything special to do, but because I wanted to get used to my classroom and think over my objectives for the year once again. Before entering my room I noticed a long line of teachers in front of the ditto machine, probably making up busywork for the kids. Why don't they just walk into the classroom without any materials and let the kids develop their own? I thought. Well, it wasn't my place to tell them how to teach, everyone has their own style. On my desk was a memo to pick up my class list from the teachers' lounge.

The teachers' lounge was next to my room. I walked into a thick haze of smoke. Most of the teachers were in small groups discussing their new students. Portelli was standing by the refrigerator moaning about some kid named Cassandra Fulton.

"Wouldn't you know it. You get a little experience and they start dumping bastards on you. This place sucks." He walked out of the room.

I picked up my class list and walked back to my room trying to pronounce some of the names. Kids were sensitive when it came to their names. I got as far as Gloria Jefferson on my class list when the bell rang. I quickly stepped out into the hallway to greet my new students personally. A steady crescendo of noise began to build. It became so loud that I was tempted to put my hands over my ears. Then I saw the first student to reach the second floor. He was on the run, followed by two other students who finally caught up to him halfway from my room and began to punch and kick him. One boy finally grabbed him from behind while the other punched him over and over again in the stomach. Both boys spotted me coming down the hall and ran off, leaving their victim on the ground. I bent down to help him up, but he pulled his arm away from me. "I don't need no help, man," he yelled. "I'm going to get the Stones on those motherfuckers and blow their fuckin' asses away."

I went back to my room, where by now some kids were already seated in the back. I heard one yell out, "Hey, we got a white teacher."

I thought to myself, Yes, I'm white, but not the kind of white they're used to. I understand why they can't read well, and, more important, that I can't force my values on them. I would try my damnedest to relate to their needs. In a few weeks they wouldn't even know I was white—just their friend trying to help them read and write.

The last student entered the room, and I walked in and shut the door. All the kids were seated. Some were eating sunflower seeds and spitting them on the floor, others were sucking on big dill pickles. That was probably their only breakfast. I would clean up the seeds later. No point making an issue of it; the kids could probably perform better with some food in their stomachs.

I picked up my roll book, walked around in front of

the desk, and sat on it. They were all looking at me intently, and the room was very quiet. Instead of calling the names off the roll in alphabetical order like most teachers did, I thought it would be better to have each student introduce himself. This would prevent me from embarrassing anyone by pronouncing his name wrong, and would also show my new students that in this classroom the students and not the teacher would be the main participants in the learning process.

I looked up from my book and told the kids that I wanted each student to stand up and give his name and where he lived and then sit down. "Be sure you say your name distinctly so that everyone in the room will know who you are."

The first student stood up and announced that her name was Darcia Ames and she lived in the projects across the street. The second student stood up and said her name was Vanessa Reed. While she was saying her name I thought to myself that teaching in an inner-city school was a snap. I already pictured myself following in the steps of John Holt and Herbert Kohl. I might even write a book and discuss some of the methods that made me a success in the inner city.

The third student had risen to give her name when the boy next to her said, "Man, why don't you give us your mama's name?"

She shot back, "At least I got a mama." All of a sudden both students were nose to nose, each calling the other a dirty motherfucker.

The whole class was standing, yelling, "We want a fight."

I stepped forward to calm the tempers when the front door opened and a short, light-skinned girl with a huge

Afro walked in. My attention was on the impending fight, so I turned quickly and asked her if she was in this class.

She said, "Yeah, I'm late."

Now standing between the two students who were still yelling profanities at each other, I said, "Would you please take a seat in the back of the room. I'll be with you in a minute."

"Get fucked, white man," she said. "I'll sit where I goddam please." She then walked over to my desk and sat in my chair.

Just at that moment I heard a desk overturn and saw two boys really punching it out in the back. I pushed the two students I was holding into their chairs and told my new student to go to the office. Then I went to the back of the room to stop the fight. One boy was hanging on my "Famous Blacks" bulletin board and the other boy was trying to pull him off. I reached both of them just as the one holding on to the board was pulled loose, ripping down my whole display.

I grabbed him. He looked up at me and said, "Don't you ever touch me, motherfucker, or my brother will come up and blow your white ass away."

I told him to get down to the office. I grabbed the other boy and was bringing him to the front of the room while telling everyone to please sit down, when I saw the girl who had come in late still sitting at my desk.

"Didn't I tell you to go to the office?"

"Yeah, I went."

"How come you're back?" She handed me a note, stapled to a discipline card, which read, "Follow procedure." At this point I could feel myself losing control. I had to remain cool. I would not resort to yelling or hitting. I turned to the class just in time to meet the other student I sent down to the office. He came back with the same stapled message. I left the late student at my desk and managed to push the two fighters into seats at the front of the room. I then tried to quiet the room, which was now filled with thirty screaming students. No one even looked up at me. Two students in the back of the room began to bounce a basketball.

One girl had opened a window and was yelling out to her girl friends, "We got a white teacher."

I began to panic. I wished I had some dittos to hand to the students to get them busy so I could have time to collect my thoughts. Then I had an idea. All their lives these kids had been hit and yelled at. Maybe if I did the reverse I would throw them off balance and they would realize that I was not an authority figure but rather a friend in education. So I just sat there and looked at my students, making no move to inhibit them. The girl at the window was now yelling some profanity at a boy on the street, and the boys started playing dodge ball off my ripped-up bulletin board. I was determined to remain cool. Then I noticed a very short boy with glasses and almost no hair on his head walk over to my "We Will Learn Together" bulletin board and with a magic marker write, "Stone Run It" and "Pony Soldier" on it.

I kept staring at him and he kept writing. Was he unaware I was watching him? Then he turned around, looked at me, grinned, and continued writing on the board. Something inside me snapped. I grabbed a book off my desk and threw it at him. It crashed loudly off the bulletin board just above his head. Everyone in the class looked up at me. I stood up and began to yell louder than I had ever yelled in my life.

"All right, I want everyone in their seats now! Shut that window and get in your seat. You, with the marker. Bring it up here and then sit down in your seat. How would you boys in the back like to lose that ball?"

I could feel the adrenalin running through my body. My face must have been beet red, and I could feel my eyes coming out of my head. The kids looked at me as if I was crazy, but they all ran to their seats. Even the girl at my desk ran to a seat. The room was absolutely quiet. Thirty pairs of eyes were staring at me. I was mad at myself. I turned around and kicked the wastebasket, and papers went all over the floor.

Then one kid raised his hand and said, "What to do, Mr. Jones, what to do!"

I realized then that I had a lot to learn, and that if I ever went back to my college I would punch my professor of culturally disadvantaged children right in the mouth.

4. "Who's this Malcom X Cat?"

*D*uring the next three days at Du Sable all classes were self-contained, which meant that the students stayed in one room all ten periods with only a break for lunch. We were told that classes would begin rotating as soon as the school had enough staff to carry on a normal program.

After my first day at Du Sable I decided to prepare busywork for my class to give me some time to study the situation. It was by now obvious to me that Herbert Kohl and John Holt had left something out. This did not mean that I had given up on their methods but merely that I had to find some way of adapting their methods to my own personality. I felt that it was my fault I was unable to control the situation that first day. I thought: If only I had materials that are relevant to the kids— something to catch their interest right away and set the tone for the rest of the year. Well, I had blown it, but I was determined to recoup my losses and find materials and subjects that would capture my group.

So I went home and made up dittos which would keep the kids busy. I hoped to use my free time to study and evaluate their needs.

The first ditto I handed out was made up of multiplication problems. There was nothing complicated about them, especially for the eighth grade. The

first girl in the second row took my ditto and
threw it on the floor saying, "I ain't doin' that shit." Her
friend in back of her said she wouldn't either. I could
feel the rebellion spreading.

I kept cool and told the class that these were review
problems and that they would serve as a good warmup
for math class when they began rotating.

The girl who had thrown down the ditto then said, "I
ain't doin' that shit, and I ain't ever goin' to math class
either."

The rest of the class laughed. I asked the girl to wait
for me in the hall. She stood up and walked out the
door. I would never see her again. And, like an ass, I
had thrown out all my truant slips.

With her gone, the rest of the class began to look at
their dittos. No one took out a pencil and tried to work
the problems. Most of the class just looked at me as if I
were crazy. I said that I would help them get started by
doing the first problem, which I then put on the board.

The class had already begun talking and eating those
damn sunflower seeds. One boy in the front leaned his
head back while I was trying to get the class's attention
and spit a steady fountain of seeds into the air. I said
several times, "Class, let's all look up at the board." But
no one looked at me. Most were engaged in conversation
with their neighbor, eating, or just lying on their desks
asleep. I began to pound my record book on the desk
and a few kids responded.

One kid yelled out, "Why don't you all shut the fuck
up and give the man a chance." Everyone turned
around and looked at the board.

I called on a girl in the back of the room who must
have had a whole package of gum in her mouth. I asked

her what three times five was. She said she didn't know. I thought to myself, "Another wiseass." Then I called on the boy who was spraying the class with sunflower seeds. He said he didn't know either.

"Does anyone here know what three times five is?" No one answered. I was paralyzed. "Does anyone know what two times two is?" A girl in the back shouted out "Four."

"Mr. Jones," came a voice from the rear. "We never learned how to multiply past three." My mouth went dry. My entire lesson for the morning was these multiplication problems, and these kids didn't even know what five times three was. Oh, my God! What do I do now?

I remembered that the first day, while I was cleaning the room, I came across some old readers in the bottom of a cabinet next to my desk. I quickly collected the dittos and distributed the books. I turned to the contents and picked out the story "Man-Eating Sharks." It sounded like a high-interest story that everyone would enjoy reading aloud. I told the class to turn to the story and we would read orally. I called on the first girl in the first row to begin. She hadn't found the page yet. I called on the next girl, but she was asleep. To my relief, I saw a hand go up. I called on the student.

"Man, I don't want to read, I just want to take a piss." The class began to laugh, and I began to lose control of myself again.

"All of us are going to read this story whether you like it or not."

The entire class went, "Oooooo! He mad now." A girl in front finally volunteered. She began reading, stumbling on every other word. "Bother" became "brother," "again" became "and," "ship" became "shit," and the class went wild. Some of the kids began to snap their books shut with a loud crack. Others just sat there looking up into the air. Then a girl in the back stood up and began to walk around. I stopped the girl who was reading and told everyone I would read the story and they should listen very carefully because I was going to give a quiz after I finished.

I began to read, but absolutely no one was listening. I stood up and was about to begin yelling when it happened: I got hit in the eye with an eraser which knocked my glasses off. Everyone abruptly took their seats as I looked up, except for one boy who was laughing and pointing at me. I took about three giant steps to his desk and jerked him out of his seat by the coat.

"Hey, man don't touch the threads! Did you hear, man? My brother's a Stone, man. He'll blow you away." I pushed him out the door. The kid struggled all the way down the hall, but I finally managed to push him into the office. An old black lady with graying hair came over to ask what the problem was. I told her that this student had hit me in the eye with an eraser.

The kid yelled at me, "You a damn liar. I never hit you. Samuel did."

The lady handed the boy a glass of water and told him to water the plants on her desk.

"Mr. Jones, are you positive that this boy hit you with an eraser?"

"Yes, I am. I saw him out of the corner of my eye."

"Are you absolutely sure?"

"Yes, I am positive."

"Mr. Jones, what were you doing in the classroom when the student hit you with the eraser?"

"I was reading a story to the class."

"Was it an interesting story?"

"I thought so," I answered lamely.

"The reason I ask you this question is that many incidents such as this could be avoided if the children were motivated. After all, a motivated child is a child out of mischief."

I kept my temper and informed her that no matter what was going on in that classroom, that boy had no right to hit me with an eraser.

"You are perfectly correct, Mr. Jones. I was just trying to explain to you the possible cause of the accident."

"What are you going to do with the boy?" I asked.

"Well, since this is his first offense, I will talk with him and have him apologize to you. Then I will drop the matter unless you want to pursue it further."

By then I had cooled down and began to think that maybe it was my fault that the incident had occurred. Why make an enemy of the kid? I thought. I'll let it drop at an apology.

"No, I'm satisfied with just an apology."

"Good, Mr. Jones, I think that is the best thing to do now." I began to leave when she called me back.

"Mr. Jones, may I make a suggestion?"

"Yes, I would appreciate any help I can get."

"Many new teachers forget that they are teaching blacks who have a different culture than whites. What might interest you will not interest them. Try to be relevant. The children will be more attentive to things they can identify with in their own cultural background. Perhaps a little discussion of Martin Luther King or Malcolm X."

I shook my head in agreement and began walking back to my classroom thinking that she was right and that once again I had let my kids down. What was relevant about man-eating sharks? I had had a couple of hours of black history in college; for the rest of the morning I decided I would discuss Malcolm X and Black Nationalism.

When I walked into the classroom everyone was running around the room and a boy was beating up a girl on top of my desk. One boy was sitting in his desk with five desks stacked on top of him so he couldn't possibly get out. As soon as I walked in, everyone ran to their seats. I guess they could see that I was still mad and that it would be best not to tempt fate any further.

I went over to my desk and sat down on the edge of it. For the first time in two days the entire class was looking at me—and quietly. I couldn't see a dill pickle in sight.

"Class, in the few minutes we have before lunch I thought we might discuss Malcolm X." Their faces remained blank. "He was a Black Muslim who, as all of you know, broke away from the Muslim religion and adopted a new set of principles. From your reading, what do you think of a man like Malcolm X?"

No one responded. They just stared blankly into my face. Students began to eat again and some began to talk.

"Does anyone want to volunteer an answer, or shall I be forced to call on someone?" No one answered. Finally a boy in the back raised his hand and said, "Mr.

Jones, who is this Malcolm X cat?" My mouth went dry again.

"How many in this class do not know who Malcolm X is?" The entire class raised their hands. I then realized that I had better talk with Portelli or for that matter any teacher in the back of the room or I was going to catch hell this year.

5. "In the Event...."

*O*n the morning of the fifth day at Du Sable I received a memo in my mailbox that there would be a teachers' meeting that morning. I was jubilant because it meant the kids would come a half-hour later than usual—and by Friday I desperately needed a rest from my class. I went up to my room where the meeting was going to be held and sat in the same desk I had sat in for the orientation meeting.

As the teachers began to come in I noticed some new faces and missed some older ones. The younger teachers again migrated to the front of the room and the older teachers remained in the back. There was a noticeable change in the attitude of both groups. The younger teachers looked like hell. Instead of a paperback book hanging out of their back pocket, there was now a soiled handkerchief. I heard no discussions about revolutions or Bakunin but rather a deadening silence sometimes interrupted by the question, "How are your classes?"

Either the answer was, "Oh, things could be better," or there was no answer at all, just a weak smile which seemed to mean that the teacher was too enfeebled for even a brief reply.

In contrast to this dismal atmosphere, the teachers in the back were laughing and joking about some of their students' attempts to act up and how they had disciplined them. Many of the older teachers seemed to get a bang out of telling stories about their new young protégés.

Coach Mills and the mustachioed teacher I had met the first day were laughing about some young teacher on the second floor who had been chased out of his room by his students. When he had returned with the principal, the kids had thrown his briefcase and overcoat out the window.

"Coach," said the mustachioed teacher, "he probably was teaching the kids the law of gravity, and they used anything available to test the theory."

"If I was teaching gravity to these bastards," roared the coach, "I'd drop one of those sons of bitches out the window and hope to hell he lands on his head."

I was offended by their jokes about something that I didn't consider funny. But after the four days I had just put in I needed to laugh at something. Maybe such levity kept these men sane. In fact I felt better after hearing the story, because now I knew that I wasn't the only one having trouble. I was about to lean over to talk to Portelli when the principal walked in and asked for quiet. I felt sure that Simpson would spend most of the meeting discussing discipline problems and ways to alleviate them. He would probably tell us how to remove students with psychological problems and what procedures to use in order to transfer maladjusted students to special schools. My depression began to diminish as Simpson started the meeting.

"Good morning, teachers. I hope all of you have begun an education program and have diagnosed your classes' needs. In the event you are not having a rewarding experience in your classroom, I would

34

suggest you check your bulletin boards for their ability to motivate and, most important, your lesson plan book to see if you are carrying out your objectives. Incidentally, Mr. De Neal has spot-checked the record books and already has noticed carelessness. I can't stress to you how important these books are. Your teacher rating will be determined largely on your ability to keep neat records. Need I say more? Now if there aren't any questions I would like all teachers to report to Room 176 where Miss McGovern will have a demonstration on how to make a bulletin board that motivates and instructs."

"Mr. Simpson," one long-haired teacher sitting in the front called out. "I am having some difficulty controlling my students. Would it be possible to discuss this problem right now?"

Thank God someone has the balls to bring up the subject, I thought. I can't believe that Simpson is going to dismiss the meeting without saying one thing about discipline. What the hell is going on around here? The administration must know that some of us younger teachers are having a hell of a time.

"Mr. Hicks," replied Simpson, "I'm glad you brought the subject up."

Goddammit, Simpson is always glad someone brings up something. Why the hell doesn't he bring up something once in a while besides those damn bulletin boards? I fumed to myself.

"It has been my experience that most discipline problems arise when the instructional program either fails to meet the needs of the student, or it lacks diversity. In other words, your choice of materials should be more varied. Let me ask you this question,

35

Mr. Hicks. Have you used a filmstrip yet?"

"No, Mr. Simpson. My room has no shades or blinds, and none of the projectors is working."

"I was not aware that all of our projectors were broken." Simpson turned his head toward a short black man with a crew cut standing near the front wall. "Mr. Franklin, I was not informed of any broken projectors."

"Mr. Simpson, I gave you the report yesterday. You told me to lay it on your desk."

"Oh, yes, I remember now. I think I sent it to District. Just exactly how do we stand?"

"Well, Mr. Simpson, I'm tinkering around with two projectors we have, hoping to fix them. If we send them downtown to get repaired, it takes about six months to get them back. If I get lucky and fix both of them, then we can get some type of scheduling program which would allow each teacher a shot at one of the two projectors. But I'm sure that if we all cooperate, sharing two projectors among eighty teachers shouldn't be too difficult. In regard to the shade problem, I have nothing to do with that. But I think the chief engineer would be the best person to talk to."

"Pardon me, Mr. Franklin," interrupted Simpson, "but I have already talked with the engineer about the shade problem and he has made out the appropriate requisition forms to be sent downtown. So, hopefully, in two or three months we can get that taken care of. Until the projectors are fixed, the audio-visual part of your lesson should be replaced by a visual program using dittos as the medium. When I was in the classroom I found many ways to motivate the children with dittoed cartoons and narrative stories with accompanying pictures."

36

"Mr. Simpson," interrupted Hicks, "the ditto machine is broken too."

"Excuse me, Mr. Simpson," came a voice from the rear. "If you stick a spoon in the side of the machine where the clamp on the knob is, and have someone hold it there, the machine runs fairly well."

A broad grin broke out on Simpson's face. "Thank you, Mr. Clips, for that bit of advice. I'm sure every teacher will remember to pack a spoon in his briefcase along with his plan book tomorrow." Simpson's attempt at levity did not produce so much as a giggle from the faculty. In fact, the only one in the room who was smiling was Simpson. He must have felt self-conscious about it because his grin mechanically disappeared after he surveyed his sullen faculty.

"Well, if there are no more questions I think we can disperse and prepare ourselves for our first day of rotation."

"Mr. Simpson," Hicks had his hand up again. "I still have not heard any suggestions on what to do with kids who are acting out and refuse to behave no matter what is done with them."

You could hear Coach Mills rumble from the back, "Kick the kid in his black ass."

"Mr. Hicks," answered Simpson in an annoyed tone, "you are seeking a definite answer to a question that does not have a definite answer. As I was trying to explain earlier, the teacher who is having problems in the classroom should first look at his instructional program. The teacher should ask himself the question, 'Is this lesson one in which the student can get involved?' "

"Mr. Simpson," interrupted Hicks. "I have made up

lesson plans and tried every possible method of interesting my students, but some of them don't give me a chance, not even a chance. Yesterday I walked into my room and began distributing my dittos and several students just threw them on the floor and others ripped them up. The rest of the class followed their example. I had complete chaos in the room. I must have spent two days developing those dittos, and before I had a chance to even explain their objective they were on the floor and the class was up for grabs!"

"Pardon me, Mr. Hicks. But, if you are faced with such behavior and you are sure that it does not originate with your educational program, then you should follow the discipline procedure as set down in the Teacher Handbook."

"But, Mr. Simpson, that procedure takes so long and there are so many forms to fill out. The problems I've faced so far required immediate action."

The argument was heating up, and I could tell that Hicks wasn't going to let up and that Simpson was trying his damnedest not to talk directly to the problem of discipline. I thought: Why is he afraid to admit that the problem exists? Can he really believe that lesson plans will prevent most of our problems?

"Mr. Simpson," came a voice from the rear. It was the mustachioed teacher who hung around with Portelli.

"Yes, Mr. Feinberg."

"I think Mr. Hicks is trying to say what a lot of us have been trying to say for years, and that is there are many kids in this school who are criminals. They have been in and out of reform schools, and they just don't belong in the classroom. But because of state laws we must accept them and tolerate them. I can't believe that any type of lesson plan or bulletin board will calm these students down. I think we all should set up a definite discipline procedure to deal with the student who refuses to learn for whatever reason, and then get on to the business of educating those people who want to learn."

"Mr. Feinberg, I respect your opinion," Simpson said, "but I don't believe that our discipline problems can be solved in such a cut and dried manner. What I have tried to implement at Du Sable is a flexible discipline procedure where every student is treated as an individual. When a child walks into this office I want him to be listened to and through our counseling staff find out what are the root causes of this student's behavior problem."

"But, Mr. Simpson, that type of service takes a lot of time. In the meantime our rooms are in a mess. Besides that, the counselors just send the kid back with a note saying to follow procedure or talk to the student in our spare period. Mr. Simpson, you know as well as I do that there are students in this school who have spent most of their time in the counseling office and nothing is ever done. Ultimately the student always returns to the class where the teacher must deal with him."

Feinberg's voice was getting louder and louder. Everyone could sense he was mad and getting madder. It also seemed that he had been through this dialogue before and knew it was futile. The back of the room was alive now. They were listening intently to the exchange. Some new hands had risen and some teachers tried to cut into Feinberg's conversation.

"Mr. Feinberg, our time is running out and we must get to our classrooms. What you have said bears some investigation, so I will appoint a committee to study the matter and perhaps it can come up with some proposals."

Voices began to yell out: "We're sick of committees." "Studies are bullshit." But Simpson held his ground and dismissed the meeting, then left the room quickly. The teachers in the back of the room stood up slowly and walked out in groups of two and three, deeply engrossed in conversation. The new teachers looked confused. They didn't know which side to join. When the bell rang their confused look changed quickly to a look of anguish. The kids were coming with their sunflower seeds, their gum, their knives, their popcorn bags, and their dislike of school and everything in it. All my colleagues and I had to combat them with was a plan book and a goddam bulletin board.

6.

"Mr. Feinberg, you are mistaken"

*M*y first period assignment after division was hall patrol. Out of ten periods in the day, every teacher was given one preparation period and one duty post. The teacher's manual which we were given on our first day at Du Sable said that a teacher on hall patrol duty should "actively supervise" the halls during the passing intervals between classes and check all students for passes at other times. Any student without a pass should be sent outside or brought to the office. I was amused by this job description, because it had been my experience while student teaching that hall patrol was a goof-off period. Most teachers never showed up at their posts, and those who did used the time to grade papers. But I decided that Simpson might be petty enough to check up on the first day, so I reported to my post which was right outside the main office and next to the gym.

The bell rang. I let out my division, picked up my record book and my plan book, and proceeded to my duty post. My room was on the second floor and my post was on the first. As I reached the stairwell I looked down the stairs at the first-floor hallway. All I could see were hundreds of kids running around, fighting, and playing dodge ball against the wall. Some were hanging on classroom doors yelling obscenities at teachers inside. I saw a group of boys with big leather hats and

43

black leather jackets near the rest rooms grabbing kids and going through their pockets for money. I was afraid to walk down the stairs.

Then I saw Portelli come out of his room on the first floor yelling, "It sucks!" at Feinberg, who was standing by the office holding a window pole in his hand. He was using the pole like an electric cattle prod to herd the kids to class. The presence of these two teachers gave me the courage to walk down the stairs.

Just before I reached the bottom steps the two big iron doors in front of the gym burst open and Coach Mills strode out with a paddle in one hand and a baseball bat in the other yelling, "I want all black ass out of this hallway. Now." With that he began grabbing kids, throwing them up against the wall, and giving them a shot on the ass with the paddle. Kids began to scatter. All I could see were coats flying, kids screaming, and Coach Mills hitting anything that came within his reach. Some kids were trying to explain to the coach why they were in the hallway, but in vain. They received the standard reply, "Get your ass out of here," followed by a shot in the ass. With his window pole Feinberg had pinned against the wall a student who was carrying an iron pipe. I thought it best to help him because Coach Mills seemed to need no help at all and Portelli was still at the end of the hall yelling repeatedly at the top of his lungs, "It sucks!"

When I reached Feinberg he was telling the kid to drop the pipe and go to the office. The kid was threatening to kill him when he left school. I tapped Feinberg on the shoulder and he swung around with the pole, stopping abruptly when he saw that I was a teacher and not a student. "Can I help?" I asked him.

44

"Yeah. Take this little bastard into the office and wait there until I come back. I left my class alone, and God knows who's in the room now."

Feinberg then released the student to me. "Whatever you do, don't turn your back on him and don't let go of him. He's gotten away a couple of times on me, but now I got the slippery bastard. Don't let him out of your sight." With that, Feinberg turned from me, lowered his window pole in front of him, and, like a knight ready to begin a joust, walked towards the school library where his class waited.

As I watched him charge into the mass of students fleeing Coach Mills, the kid whom I had by the arm jerked loose and began to run. I caught him by his long coat and I heard it rip. "Hey, man, watch the threads! You got no right ripping my threads, man." I pulled him into the office where I was met by a long line of students standing by the counter waiting for their late passes to be signed. The bench in front of the counter was filled with students talking, laughing, and eating those damn sunflower seeds. I brought the boy around the counter to a counselor who informed me that she didn't handle such cases and directed me to the Master Teacher who informed me that he did not handle such cases and directed me to the vice-principal who was deeply engrossed in conversation with two policemen. I stood there for a couple of minutes, trying to make my presence felt in subtle ways, when I heard some loud bangs in the hallway which sounded like firecrackers. The entire office fell silent.

One of the policemen turned towards the door. "Jesus! That sounded like gunshots."

The two policemen, the principal, and I dashed out

45

into the hallway. We ran around the gym towards the
library just in time to meet Feinberg as he charged out
of his room with his window pole and his eyes bulging
out of his head.

"Shit, I heard four gunshots go off, Mr. Barber."

"Mr. Feinberg," replied the vice-principal, "you are
mistaken. There was only one shot."

This reply seemed to startle Feinberg so that he
could not get his next sentence out. He just looked at us,
shook his head, turned around, and went back into his
room. I was curious to hear what he was going to say.
He started to move his lips, but Barber's statement
stopped him cold. The policemen began checking the
walls for bullet holes; Barber turned around, shook his
head at me, and left; and I, remembering that I had left
that kid alone in the office, ran back and found that
Feinberg was right. He was slippery. I walked back into
the hallway and sat in a chair by the gym. The two
steel doors of the gym opened again and there stood the
coach. He looked up and down the hall and then
directly at me.

"Was there a shooting out here?"

"Yes," I replied.

"Did anyone get killed?"

"No."

"Goddammit. You'd think these sons of bitches would
hit each other once in a while. Shit, these kids aren't
just stupid, they're bad shots, too. They can't do
anything right." He glanced up and down the hall again
and then stepped back into the gym.

I glanced at my watch. It had taken Coach Mills,
Feinberg, from one to four gunshots, two policemen,
and a principal twenty-five minutes to clear the hallway

46

of kids. But it was finally clear and quiet. I had begun
to enjoy it when a voice broke my solitude.

"Hello, my name is Mr. Portelli."

I looked up and extended my hand. "My name is
Mr. Jones."

"Is this your hall patrol post?" Portelli asked.

"Yeah. It is."

"Well, at least they put two men down here. Last
year I was stationed down there," Portelli pointed
towards the other end of the hall, "with a woman, and it
really got bad. Some of these dudes would come up. . . .
Well, I won't get into it, you'll find out soon enough."

"Is it always this bad when the periods change?"
I asked.

"Yes. You can expect the halls to be like this every
period, except for that shooting which was out of the
ordinary. Usually these bastards shoot it up in the
playground. At least that's what happened last year.
One time I was coming across the parking lot when
these two gangs turned it into the O.K. Corral. There
were gunshots all over the place."

"What did you do?"

"I got my ass out of there in a hurry, that's what I did.
But like I said, this is the first time they shot it up in
the hallway to my knowledge. Who knows what these
crazy bastards are going to do next?"

"Just exactly what are we supposed to do on this hall
duty post?" I asked Portelli.

"You're supposed to check for passes and keep the
high school kids from coming through this wing to get
out to the playground. That's what we're supposed to do
officially. Actually, you sit your ass down in a desk and
hope the hell one of these big dudes doesn't decide to

come over to the desk and knock you out of it. Whatever you do, be careful who you try to stop from going through these hallways. You're new, and I know at first you're going to try to do your job. Well, that's all right. But if one of those high school kids gives you any lip—which they will—take it and walk away. Because I won't back you up. These kids are tough, and you don't know what they're carrying. All you need is to jam some gangbanger (active gang member) who's been drinking wine all night, and you might find yourself dead. So best leave the big ones alone, even if they call you a motherfucker.

"Now, if Coach Mills is out here, that's a different ball game. These bastards are scared shitless of him, and you can make these kids do right if he's in the hall. But if he's not in the hall you get humble real fast."

Portelli turned from me and glanced down the hall. "Goddammit, you better stand up, here comes the District Superintendent. First time I've seen the bastard since last year. I think he's afraid to come out of his office."

I quickly stood up and moved next to Portelli as if both of us were actively supervising the hall. The District Superintendent was a short, stocky, white man who waddled when he walked. When he reached us he nodded his head and began to pass, then stopped and turned around, hand extended.

"Hello. My name is Mr. Borden."

I introduced myself. He asked me if I was new and I said yes.

"Well, I hope you like Du Sable. The main thing here is not to get hurt. Be careful young man." With that he patted me on the shoulder, shook hands with Portelli, and vanished out the door.

"Boy, do I wish I had his job," said Portelli. "He sits on his can all day sending out directives, telling us how to motivate these bastards, and doesn't even walk into the classroom. What a piece of cake!"

"If things are so bad and he's warning me not to get hurt, why the hell doesn't he do something about it?" I asked.

"Because he doesn't want to rock the boat. He's a white man in a totally black school system and his job isn't the most secure. Why, last year some students knocked down his secretary, walked into his office, and presented him with some demands."

"What did he do?"

"He sat there and listened to them and gave them the stock administrative answers filled with terms like 'relevant' and 'involved.' You know how that bullshit goes. Then he sent out a directive blaming the teachers for the conditions in this hole. That bastard would do anything to keep his job, including endangering your life. This place is fuckin' dangerous and he knows it, and he isn't going to do anything about it, because if he does he'll be back in the classroom with us and that prospect is enough to kill anyone's crusading zeal. So he stays in his office, minds his own business, attends a lot of meetings downtown, and tells his bosses what a great job he's doing and what a shitty job we're doing. Once in a while he sends out memos telling us that things could be better if we were more sympathetic to the students' needs, and to try harder."

"Well, if he's not going to do anything, what can we

do as teachers to improve the situation?" I asked. Portelli's lower lip dropped. His mouth started to move just like Feinberg's had when Barber told him there was only one bullet fired. Finally, Portelli managed to talk.

"There's not a damn thing you can do except try to stay alive when you walk into that classroom. You do that by being tough as nails and hoping no one calls your bluff. These kids come from a tough environment. They respect tough people. If you're not tough then you'd better forget about teaching here, because these kids will turn your classroom into a living hell. But you do what you want—most new teachers find out the hard way. I'm just giving you my philosophy on teaching in the ghetto. Take it or leave it. But whatever you do, think twice before you try anything those education professors told you to do. They never taught in a situation like this and have no business telling you how it is in the ghetto. Last year we had one of those clowns come from the university, and he told me in the faculty lounge that all you need to teach these kids to read is one pack of ditto paper. Can you believe that?!"

"What happened to him?"

"Well, the kids took his one pack of ditto paper and threw it out the window, and then threw his coat and briefcase out the window. It was beautiful. But that same bastard will go back to his school and tell his students how he related in the ghetto, and he may even write a book like *Thirty-Six Children* and make a lot of bread while I'm here getting my ass kicked."

Portelli went on talking about how bad the school was when I noticed a lanky boy walking down the hall.

He was wearing a black fur coat and a big leather hat. Portelli noticed him, too, but didn't stop talking. I approached the kid, leaving Portelli behind me.

I heard Portelli say, "Don't bother him." But it was too late, I had already stepped in his path and told him to turn back. He looked at me and kept walking. I told him again to please turn around—that this was the junior high wing and he belonged in the high school wing.

He stopped right in front of me and pointed his finger at me and said, "Get fucked, man." He then proceeded to walk past me.

I decided not to press the point because he looked awfully mean and Portelli had already retreated to the gym door just in case things got out of hand. I turned around to see what door he was going out of when Mr. Jordan, one of the Master Teachers, stepped out of the main office. He was a short man, very fat. I had been told that he was a very good teacher and that this was his first year in the office.

He grabbed the boy by the arm and said, "Brother, you're not supposed to go out this door." The boy jerked his arm away from him.

"Listen, motherfucker," the boy yelled, "don't you ever touch me again or I'll bring my boys up here and blow your motherfuckin' black ass off. Do you get me? I'll kill you if you ever touch me again. Kill your ass dead." He turned and marched out of the building. Jordan looked at me and shrugged his shoulders, and walked back into the office. I looked over at Portelli just as the bell rang. His face had no expression on it, just a blank look which seemed to be a characteristic reaction of all the older teachers to any event in the school, good or bad. I grabbed my books and turned to go upstairs to class.

"Jones!" yelled Portelli, as I was being engulfed by students leaving their first period class. I turned and saw Portelli standing on the bottom step of the stairway, elevating himself above the confusion.

"Yeah," I yelled.

"It sucks."

7.
"Understand?"

*M*y first class after hall patrol was language arts with Division 204 in Room 208, which was located on the second floor. As I pushed my way through the hall, alternately stepping over students who were fighting and dodging basketballs which were being thrown at other students, I was trying to think of a way to approach my new class. Should I be tough as nails as Portelli suggested and Coach Mills acted, or should I try to be friendly towards my new students, hoping they would accept me as their partner in learning? All my instincts preferred the latter, yet all my experiences at Du Sable so far seemed to point to the former. Maybe I should try to blend these two approaches. No, Du Sable was a school of extremes, and any kind of blending would be a dangerous enterprise: there would be no second chance if the particular blend I chose failed. Whatever I did would have to be total and deliberate. I would have to be committed to it no matter what happened. The problem was which method to use. As I entered Room 208 to find the students throwing books and erasers at each other, my perplexity ended. The only thing that would get these kids in their seats and stop them from killing each other was Coach Mills, and Coach Mills it would be.

I stood in the doorway, but no one noticed me except

a short, undernourished dark girl wearing a dirty ribbed dress. She ran up to me as soon as I entered and handed me a note. I opened the note and it read:

Teacher,

Please excuse Annette because she was stabbed in the back and has to spend a few days in the hospital.

Mr. A. Samson.

I looked down at the girl and asked her who she was.

"Oh, I'm Shirley, Annette's girl friend. She ain't coming to school until she be well. The Cobrettes got her. They be pretty bad." Shirley then turned and went back to a seat which wasn't in the line of fire of flying erasers and books.

I needed a dramatic way to catch the kids' attention and tell them that I meant business. I walked to my desk with only a few students noticing that I had entered the room. No one had stopped throwing books and erasers, even those who had noticed me. I began to yell, but that did not seem very dramatic. Then I spotted a wastebasket next to my desk. I approached it and kicked it clear across the room; it bounced off the far wall spilling papers all over the floor. The entire class stopped throwing things and ran for their seats except for a tall, thin boy in the back of the room with an enormous Afro. As he slowly walked towards me, I could sense the entire class's eyes on us. I felt like Gary Cooper in the showdown scene from *High Noon*. The boy reached me and just looked me up and down.

"Hey, man, wha' ya kick that pail for, man? No reason to kick that pail like that, man."

"Young man, take your seat."

"Hey, man, you be telling me . . ."

56

Before he reached the end of his sentence I grabbed him by the collar and with all my strength banged him against the wall. His eyes almost came out of his head in disbelief. He looked scared—which startled me—but I kept him against the wall.

"I asked you once to get in your seat, and I don't ask people twice to do something in my class. Is that clear? My name is Mr. Jones and not 'man.' So either get in your seat or get out."

I released him and he went to sit down in a seat in the back. I was lucky and I knew it. I took a big chance with that boy, because if he had slugged me I could have never walked back into the classroom. I turned around to be greeted by thirty faces who were waiting for my next move. I walked over to the desk and sat on it.

"My name is Mr. Jones. I'm your language arts teacher for the year. I'll tell you right now, I never want to see anyone in this room throwing anything, not even paper into that pail over there. When I come to this room I expect everyone to be in their seats and ready to work. If you want to fool around or throw things, do it on the playground—not in here, because if you do it in here then you're going to answer to me. Is that clear? This year is going to be good or bad depending on how you act. If you want to learn and get something out of school, then I'm ready and willing to help you. If you want to fool around and screw up in class, then I'm ready and able to make this classroom a living hell for you. Are there any questions?"

I then wrote an exercise on the board and told them to begin it while I checked their names and assigned them seats. I sat down at the teacher's desk and could feel myself shaking. My hands were wet with perspiration. The class had tested me, and at least for now I had won the initial battle. I couldn't believe it. All my students had their pencils out and were doing the assignment. You could hear a pin drop. I was still trying to figure out where I had gotten the words for the speech I had just made when I heard a knock at the door. I got out of my seat and went to the door. There were a bunch of older-looking boys making faces at my class. When they saw me, they gave me the finger and yelled through the door, "Suck my dick," and ran away.

Thank God for that, I thought.

I had just seated myself when I heard another knock at the door. This time I didn't pay any attention to it. But whoever it was kept knocking. I stood up just as the knocker opened my door and walked in.

"My name is Snowden. Let's see. You have one desk, one conference table, one conference chair . . ."

He went on with what I supposed was an inventory of the room. I thought it a little rude of him to tell me only his name. At least he could have told me who he was and what he was doing. He asked me to sign a sheet, then walked to the door and opened it and left. I turned around to go back to my desk when I heard the door open again.

"Jones!" It was Snowden again. "Don't ever leave your door unlocked. Understand?"

"I don't have a key," I answered.

"Well, get one and lock up. Understand?" The door shut abruptly.

I didn't sit down again because the way things had gone thus far there would have to be at least one more interruption. I was not disappointed. This time it was a white teacher with long black hair and a mustache.

"Hello, my name is Mr. Shapiro and I'm your A.V. Coordinator." He handed me a slip and I signed a paper on a clipboard he was carrying. He turned and left without another word. I opened the slip to find that the following films were available this week:

1. *Buddhist World*
2. *Claudius, Boy of Ancient Rome*

I was not much impressed with the film selections this week, but since my room had no shades or blinds and none of the projectors were working, it really didn't matter what films they had downstairs. I walked over to the pail I had kicked and brought it back to my desk where I threw my first memo away. Then I heard another knock at the door. It was Snowden again.

"My name is Mr. Snowden. Let's see—you have one desk, one . . ." He stopped, looked up at me, and smiled, "I was already here. Excuse me." At the door he turned. "Jones, don't leave your door unlocked. Understand?"

Yes, I understood.

8.

"Cover Yourself"

*A*fter a few weeks at Du Sable I had changed enough to survive. This meant that I could walk into my classes and expect to leave them in the same condition I entered—in one piece. At the same time, being safe in my class did not mean I was absolutely safe, only relatively safe. I still had to walk in the halls, and unless you were Coach Mills there was always somebody in those dark, musty corridors who could and would do you bodily harm. Some of those "gangbangers" would like nothing better than to tell their boys how they ripped off some honky teacher in school today. "Man, you should have seen that white motherfucker go down."

Hall patrol was not as frightening because Portelli showed me where I could hide during my hall guard period and the excuses to use if I were caught. When we did report to our duty posts we remained inconspicuous by walking up and down the hallway, popping into exit vestibules and the main office for a couple of minutes. This evasive maneuver, as Portelli explained it, would not keep us in one place for any length of time, thus avoiding confrontations with students. It also appeared that we were "actively supervising the halls."

At first the change in my classroom style and the devious maneuvers I used on hall patrol seemed contemptible—a gross abdication of all the values I had cherished in college and had decided to pattern my life after. But Du Sable demanded one value that college didn't—safety. Consequently, along with my new colleagues, I was forced by my new environment not only to consider my safety but to put it above all the intellectual principles I had developed at college.

I began to realize that the older teachers around me were not cynics but realists. They were surviving as best they could in a strange environment where only the strongest were respected and allowed to remain. This was a startling discovery for me and for my younger colleagues, whose middle-class backgrounds and training had made safety banal—something one thought about when he crossed the street or verbalized only as rhetoric in a society fascinated by apocalyptic visions.

Safety would keep you alive at Du Sable—nonetheless it would not secure your job. To be considered a "good teacher" at Du Sable meant you had to look and act like any other teacher would under normal circumstances. But Du Sable was no normal school, a fact which I did not realize at first. This inability on my part to face realities made my first months at Du Sable difficult at best. I was working twice as hard as any other teacher and earning the most criticism. This apparent incongruity made me double my efforts, only to receive double the criticism in return. What was I doing wrong? Couldn't the administration see all the work I was doing? Only time and experience would give me the answer to these questions and a way of dealing with them which subtly paralleled my maneuvers on hall patrol.

The first experience I had with what I thought was a routine circumstance occurred after about a month at Du Sable. Several of my students were truant. I filled out the appropriate slips and sent them to our attendance officer. I received no reply. Truancy, in my opinion, was a serious offense. So I decided to check into the reason for the lack of feedback from my inquiries. I was told by a Master Teacher in the main office to keep sending out the slips even though I received no answer. When I pressed her further on the reason why I was not receiving any answers, she replied that she didn't know either, but to keep sending out the slips because "At least you'll be covering yourself."

I let the subject drop there, because she was becoming irritated with my questions and maybe she didn't know why I wasn't receiving any replies. Still, I was annoyed at doing something that bore no results, except that of "covering myself," whatever that meant.

Coming out of lunch a week later, I was introduced to the attendance officer, Mr. Means. I immediately informed him that I had sent several truant notices to him and had received no reply.

"My box number is 179."

"I know what your box number is, Mr. Jones," replied Means.

"Then why haven't I received any replies?"

He looked at me and gave me a big smile. "I can tell you right now that all of those students you sent slips on are truant."

"Now what do I do?" I asked.

"Nothing, just keep sending out those slips. After all, you have to cover yourself."

"You mean you can't make those kids come back to school?"

"Listen, Mr. Jones," said Means, "I'm lucky that I get back here after checking some of those dudes out, much less worrying about bringing them back. Why, just yesterday I was attacked by some mother who told me her kid didn't want to go to school and to get fucked. The only thing I can do is make out a report and put it on the court docket, which is already three years behind. By the time these kids are brought to court they are of legal age. Consider yourself lucky that all you have to do to cover yourself is make out a slip. I have to go over to those projects and question the parents in order to make out my report, and believe me, that's one hell of a way to cover yourself."

The other attendance problem I had was cutting. In the morning I would have perfect attendance, but in the afternoon half of my division would cut out, missing their language arts and math classes. The teachers of these classes sent me yellow slips which informed me of this situation. I was determined to stop this cutting and receive no more yellow slips from those teachers.

The morning after I received my first yellow slip I announced to my class that I would not tolerate cutting, and if it continued the offenders would be sent to the office. This threat was met with apathetic looks from my class. After several days' worth of yellow slips, I decided to act. I wrote down all those who had cut more than three times and put the list in my desk. The next morning I sent those students to the office with a note explaining their offense. I had not finished with the roll when they returned from the office with big grins on

64

their faces and a note which read, "Follow procedure."

After division I went straight to the office and asked Snowden why he hadn't disciplined the students I had sent down. His head tipped to one side as it always did when he began to speak.

"Jones, it is the responsibility of the teacher to take care of cutting. Understand?"

"What can I do as a teacher to stop cutting?" I replied.

"Have you looked in your Du Sable Teacher's Manual?"

"Yes, I have. But the procedure there seems so long and complicated, and I want these kids to stop cutting as soon as possible. That's why I brought the case to you."

Snowden leaned back in his chair, tilting his entire body in the direction of his already tilted head, and picked a huge apple off his desk. He wrapped his mouth around it and bit in, taking fully half of it in one bite. Juice dripped down his chin and onto his suit coat.

"Jones," Snowden said as he chewed on the apple, "your job is to follow procedure, and that way you will be covering yourself. That's all that should concern you. Understand?"

It was a bit difficult to understand what he was saying because of the apple in his mouth. But I had heard the words "cover yourself," and that meant the discussion had ended. I hurried back to my students, who were cutting at that very moment. I was convinced that I would have to go through the proper channels to get any action.

The Du Sable Teacher's Manual said that cuts were detrimental to the student's progress, and therefore should be dealt with in the following manner.

First, the students should be told about their cuts and

informed of the consequences if such behavior continued. I had already done this, so I could proceed to the second step—calling the parents. This proved ineffective because most of the phone numbers I called were false and those that were correct were answered by some cousin, aunt, or younger sister who couldn't tell me when the mother would be home or for that matter whether a mother existed.

My next step was to mail a letter to the parents. This proved equally ineffective because I received half the letters back stamped "Change of address, destination unknown." The other half were never returned. I found out later that the reason for this lack of response was either that the student had destroyed the letter or that his parents didn't care.

I did receive one response for my efforts. This occurred a week later while I was "teaching" my language arts class. There was a knock at the door and, being accustomed to this sort of interruption, I quickly opened it and went back to my class, expecting whoever it was to wait by the door until I had finished giving the assignment. Instead, a young lady wearing a waitress's uniform entered the room, staggered to my desk, and began cursing at me. I grabbed her by the arm and ushered her out of the room. She leaned against the corridor wall outside in an attempt to balance herself. I could smell whiskey on her breath, and I realized that this was not going to be a textbook parent interview.

"Are you the man that keeps sending those letters to me about my son, Harold?"

"Yes, I am."

"Well, I'm going to tell you something, I don't want

you doin' that no more. My boy is good. He just don't
like school and you be sending that policeman around
and those letters. I don't want it no more. Understand?"

"I'm sorry if I have inconvenienced you, but it's my
job to send those slips out. The state authorizes me
to keep tabs on your son's attendance."

"Listen, man, I told you I don't want no more letters
and no more cops."

I began sweating and almost told her that I was only
covering myself and that she had covered herself by
appearing, so let's forget the whole thing. Instead, I kept
informing her of my duties. After all, I was only taking
orders. Couldn't she understand that? Every attempt
at explaining my reasons was met with the same reply,
"No cops and no letters." After about ten minutes she
stopped talking and walked away muttering to herself,
"No cops, no letters."

I went back into my room muttering, "I've got to get
out of here."

My final assault on the cutting problem was a trip to
Simpson's office. I told him what I had done and the
resistance I had met. He told me that if I had complied
with all the steps in the Teacher's Manual, that's all
that could be expected of me. There was no mention of
covering myself because Simpson was principal and
above such vulgar terms. Better to ask me if I had
complied with all the steps, thus cleverly covering
himself.

Our plan books were collected every Tuesday for
inspection by Simpson. He really believed that a good
plan book meant good teaching, and vice versa. (For
those interested in administrative procedures, this

67

fetish for neat and complete plan books was an excellent example of side-issue specialization, which Laurence J. Peter and Raymond Hull document in their book *The Peter Principle*. "Look after the molehills and the mountains will look after themselves.")

In my plan book I put down everything that went on in my classroom. It was a complete account of my futile attempts at teaching. But at least I was honest. At Du Sable honesty was not enough, as I found out. My book was rated unsatisfactory, and I was called into Simpson's office for a discussion on planning.

I arrived for my appointment a few minutes early and struck up a conversation with Mrs. King, a Master Teacher who had been very helpful to me in the past. I told her why I had been called down. She asked to see my book, which I handed to her. While she examined my plans, I explained to her that everything in the book was an accurate representation of my classroom work. She began to shake her head and cluck her tongue.

"Mr. Jones, these plans show honesty, but you failed to cover yourself."

Before I could answer her, Simpson stepped out of his office and invited me in. I took the book from Mrs. King and entered.

"Mr. Jones, you may sit over there. May I have your book? Thank you."

He paged through the book quickly and immediately referred to a notebook on his desk.

"Mr. Jones, your book only shows what you are doing in the classroom. Where are your objectives, your aims, your materials, your evaluations? Have you read the Du Sable Teacher's Manual on planning and its importance in your success as a teacher?"

I nodded yes.

"Well, then, why haven't you followed the model the manual sets down?"

I did not know what to say because the manual had specifically stated that planning was a flexible process and that the model used was only a guide. I had been trained at college to use the plan book sparingly. What could I say? The silence was broken by Simpson, who was visibly annoyed at my silence.

"Let me put it this way, Mr. Jones. When you walk into the classroom do you have an aim?"

I was about to say, "Yes, to walk out again." But this was a time for covering up, not for honesty.

"Yes, Mr. Simpson, I do have aims when I walk into the classroom, but I did not note them in my book. I'm sorry I did not follow proper procedure. In the future, I will adhere to the manual model."

Simpson's frown changed into a smile. He was now leaning over his desk listening to my excuses intently.

"Mr. Jones, that is what I am here for, to correct mistakes. Let me say that your book is not all bad. It just lacks structure, and you know how I feel about structure.

Did I.

He handed me the book and I stood up to leave.

"Mr. Jones, I noticed that in your book you did not have any audio-visual materials listed."

"Mr. Simpson, my room has no shades and none of the projectors are working. Mr. Shapiro told me it would be useless to order films because downtown had a cut in staff, which makes it almost impossible to get filmstrips."

"Pardon me, Mr. Jones, but Mr. Shapiro should not

have told you that. Certainly we are working under difficult conditions here, but that is no reason to stop planning or give up. Is it, Mr. Jones?"

I was nodding in agreement.

"Mr. Jones. The most I can expect of you and the rest of the faculty is to follow procedure, as fruitless as it may seem to you. To do anything less would betray our profession. Thank you, Mr. Jones, for your time."

As I left the office, Mrs. King winked at me with a benign look, as if to say she wished she could have shown me how to cover up my plan book before it was checked. I went back to my room and spent my lunch period covering up my mistakes. After all, I did not want to betray my profession.

After eight weeks at Du Sable I went around to each teacher to find out how my division was doing. Report cards were due out after ten weeks. Maybe I could give some of the students a pep talk before final exams. Each teacher I visited had a tale of woe to tell me about my division.

"Anthony won't stop playing with his gun."

"Tommy doesn't do anything but draw dirty pictures."

"Darlene has a mouth like the Holland Tunnel."

"Regina asked me yesterday in class if her pussy smelled."

Aside from these complaints, I was able to compile a list of students who were receiving a "U" (unsatisfactory) in all their subjects. I found after further investigation into these students' folders that all of them had very low IQ's and were almost nonreaders. Two of the students had been transferred from EMH rooms that were overcrowded. (EMH stood for Educable Mentally Handicapped—but the EMH rooms turned out to be dumping grounds for severe discipline problems, nonreaders, and so forth.) The Du Sable Teacher's Manual gave specific instructions for cases such as this. I was to make out a blue slip, which meant these students would be tested by a psychologist, diagnosed, and placed in a special classroom.

I obtained the proper forms from the office and filled them out. They were long and complicated forms to complete, but I was determined to help these kids out. Putting them in a regular classroom would only frustrate them and breed rebellion. I submitted the forms a week later, and waited for a reply. But, like all of my previous experiences, there was no reply. After a month I went to the office and asked Mrs. King why. She took me over to her desk, sat me down, and told me that there was only one psychologist for Area A schools and that she couldn't possibly visit all of them in one year. Mrs. King then leaned over me and lowered her voice.

"Mr. Jones, even if she could get to our school more often, there just isn't any room for special classrooms— or, for that matter, any teachers who are willing to teach those kids."

"Then, why," I asked, "are we instructed to fill in these slips when no action is taken on them?" That same benign look came over her face.

"Mr. Jones, just cover yourself. There is nothing you can do but protect yourself. Remember that. You're a good teacher. Don't throw that away by disregarding procedure or questioning it."

Mrs. King was right and I knew it. The entire school

was the victim of a Catch-22 which says, "They (Board, principal, Master Teachers, Snowden, and so forth) have a right to do anything we (teachers, community) can't stop them from doing." Or to put it more succinctly: We were all covering up for them to protect ourselves.

In the weeks following my discussion with Mrs. King, I did follow procedure. I gave students grades which in no way reflected their real achievement. I handed in instructional reports which were designed to show some innovative teaching method I was using. I ordered supplies and filmstrips which I knew would never arrive. I even reviewed textbooks from the Board which I knew my kids couldn't read. I did all of these jobs efficiently and according to procedure. The administration considered me a good teacher now, even though I wasn't raising my kids' reading scores or helping them learn social studies. But that was the trouble with the kids at Du Sable. They wouldn't cover themselves.

9. The Consultant

*A*n in-service meeting was held every other week at Du Sable. Classes were dismissed for an hour in the morning so the teachers could get together and listen to a consultant lecture on his area of expertise. These lectures were supposed to show us new ways of approaching our students, in hopes that new techniques would magically raise our students' math and reading scores.

I was excited about my first in-service class because everything I had done thus far at Du Sable had failed. I still held out some hope that these specialists knew what they were doing and could help to make my classroom teaching more effective. On my way to the meeting, which was held in my room, I met Portelli and Coach Mills going in the opposite direction.

"Mr. Portelli, aren't you going to the in-service meeting?" I asked.

"No. The Coach and I are going for some coffee."

"I think you should stay, Mr. Portelli. This consultant is going to talk on reading."

"The only way I'd go to those goddam meetings," the Coach bellowed, "is if they had a karate expert teach me how to break someone's back."

"Coach," said Portelli, "that's not a bad idea. You should talk to Simpson about that. He's the guy who's always talking about being relevant."

"Better yet," said the Coach, "they ought to bring in Dick Butkus as principal and commit Simpson to an institution where all he'd have to do is put up bulletin boards."

Their behavior and suggestions always involved physical violence to contain our students, and this still unnerved me. Wouldn't it be better to accomplish this objective with better lessons? I had become pessimistic about a lot of things at Du Sable, but I still believed that after I achieved discipline in the class there must be some way to improve these kids' reading scores. And since I was not trained to teach reading, the consultant might help make up for my deficiencies in this area.

Upon entering the room, I noticed a distinct change from previous meetings. The younger teachers were still sitting up front, but there were hardly any older teachers in the back of the room. This observation was also made by Simpson when he entered the room with a young, long-haired man. He sat on the edge of my desk, took out his notebook, and began to make notations in it while looking around the room.

I suspected that a lot of people would have memos in their boxes the next day—but, I thought, that's the price you pay for not covering yourself. Portelli and the rest of the experienced teachers should have known Simpson would consider this an insult to the profession. I took a seat towards the back and began thinking about Simpson's conversation with the Coach when he called him in for not attending the meeting. How would Simpson react to the Coach's suggestion of having a karate expert come to the meetings? I grinned at the prospect.

76

"Good morning, teachers. I will limit my opening comments in order to give all our language arts people the maximum benefit of our consultant, Mr. Green." Simpson reached over to pick up his notebook which he had laid on the desk in front of him. The entire room was silent as he thumbed through his book. As he continued thumbing, his eyes began to narrow, and the grin with which he had begun the meeting disappeared. He finally looked up at us with a scowl on his face. I almost started laughing, because his expression reminded me of how I must look when I entered my classes. Whatever was coming was not going to be pleasant.

"It has come to my attention," Simpson continued, "that many of you are not handing in your plan books or getting your bulletin boards up on time. Last week, for example, out of a staff of eighty, I received seventeen books—and half of those were done improperly. Yesterday morning I toured the halls, noting in my book those teachers who had put up a bulletin board in accordance with the schedule which all of you received at the beginning of the year. The results were just as dismal as the plan books. I found half the boards not up and the other half either lacking a theme or just incomplete. Might I add that a bulletin board which says 'Happy Birthday George' is not adequate. The plan book and the bulletin boards are not to be what some teachers like to call busywork. Rather, they are attempts to show how well you are progressing with your educational program. The bulletin boards, in particular, reflect the work you are doing in your class and should not reflect the teacher's artistic talents. I sent memos out to all teachers who did not comply with either one of these duties, and expected to have a private conference with each one. As yet, no one has responded to my memo. Further investigation reveals to me that many of you are not checking your mailboxes but just letting papers pile up in them. I would like to know the reason for this lack of response." No one in the room moved. "Is there any reason for this unprofessional conduct?"

Simpson glared around the room, daring anyone to raise their hand. No one seemed ready to challenge him. I figured he wouldn't say anything more because he had covered himself; now it was up to all of us to get on the stick and cover ourselves.

"I hope in the future I will not have to spend so much time on routine matters. From now on, I hope all of us will respond on time to all duties which were laid out in our first bulletin. That includes checking your mailboxes."

Simpson then shut his notebook, looked around the room once more, and began to smile again. "Will all math and science teachers report to Room 172? The rest of the staff should remain in this room where Mr. Green, our consultant, will give us an in-service on reading." Simpson then went to the back of the room, sat down, and reopened his notebook.

Mr. Green came to the center of the room and began to speak. I had taken out a piece of paper to take notes. The other teachers in the room, particularly the older ones, were in a solemn state and seemed to be just shifting their chins from hand to hand, meanwhile keeping one eye on Simpson and his notebook. After all, one wrong move (such as falling out of your desk because you were sleeping) could mean a memo and possibly an extra bulletin board for punishment.

"My name is Mr. Green and I come from Trinity College, which is located just southwest of here. Our education department has been working on a speed-reading technique for our freshmen, and its results have been so spectacular that I have been sharing it with many public schools." I was not impressed with his introduction, especially the part about his education department. That word had become a bad omen to me ever since my first day. What the hell does he mean by speed reading? I wondered. I don't give a damn how fast my kids read as long as they can read.

"Most freshmen," Green went on, "when they come to college have difficulty keeping up with the assignments because they have poor reading habits. Our department has found that the primary reason for failure in the freshman year is slow reading which results in frustration and finally dropping out. To combat this situation, all incoming freshmen have been given this reading course. Our results have been so encouraging that we decided to show the public schools our program in hopes they will use it to improve their students' reading ability."

Green then walked over to an overhead projector and began flashing letters on the wall, asking us to recall them. Then he handed out some cards which we held up to our eyes and with a partner observed each other's eye movement. Finally he handed out paperbacks to all the teachers in the room; I received *Heart of Darkness* by Joseph Conrad. We were instructed to turn to any page and practice finger movements which, according to Green, would help us increase our speed without sacrificing comprehension.

I finished before anyone, not because I was a fast reader but because I was fed up and didn't feel like playing any more games. I couldn't figure out how these kinds of exercises could help my kids read better. It seemed to me that Green's program was based on the premise that the students who take the course can *read* to begin with. At Du Sable this was too much to assume. Maybe I didn't understand what Green was trying to say. I quickly jotted down some questions on my empty note paper and hoped the question period would straighten things out. But before I could ask them, Simpson had come to the front of the room.

"Pardon me," Simpson began, "but we are running out of time. Before Mr. Green leaves, we have to decide if this program is worth another visit and possibly setting up a training session for some of our teachers at Trinity College. Are there any questions concerning Mr. Green's technique?"

I couldn't believe it: no one raised his hand. I must be losing my mind.

"Mr. Green," I yelled from the back, "what type of students have you tried this program on so far?"

"I'm glad you asked that question," Green responded. "We have some pilot programs already going in the high schools around our college, and so far the classes we have tried them on have all responded well."

"May I ask what is the reading level of these students in your pilot program?"

"All the students are in honors programs in their respective high schools. So I would say they are reading one or two years above their grade level."

"Would this program work with nonreaders, or with

students who read two or three grades below level?" This question seemed to startle Green. He looked like he had never been asked it before.

"Well," Green began to grin, "we expect that anyone who takes the course can read, at least grade level." Green laughed at his comment as if my question were ridiculous.

"Mr. Simpson, why are we even listening to this man?" I asked, outraged. (That wiped Green's smile off his face.) "None of our students are reading grade level, and, in fact, my class has many nonreaders in it. Mr. Green's program in no way seems to attack the problems we have here."

"Thank you, Mr. Jones, for your opinion," Simpson answered. "Are there any more comments?"

I was alarmed by this obvious brush-off. I felt I had made a very good point which no one seemed to acknowledge. Maybe I hadn't made myself clear. Green had just stated that this program worked only for grade-level readers, which to my knowledge did not exist at Du Sable.

"Well," Simpson broke the silence, "since there is no strong opposition to Mr. Green's program, I think it would be best if he came back next week and gave another in-service on it. Then maybe we will be able to make a better judgment. Simpson's decision brought back Green's smile, and he began to play with his overhead projector again.

Simpson dismissed us, and I walked out furious. I met Portelli in the hallway.

"Mr. Portelli, you won't believe what just happened. They might initiate a speed-reading program here for kids who are reading grade level."

"You mean we have kids here who are reading grade level?"

"That's the point. The program can't possibly work here, and yet Simpson acted as though it had some merit."

"Who knows, maybe Simpson wants to improve his speed. Don't be so discouraged, Jones. At least this has taught you a lesson."

· "What's that, Portelli?"

"Don't go to another in-service unless they have a karate expert doing it."

10. "There is No Such Creature?"

*M*idway through the year I had been able to construct, as Simpson would put it, an "ongoing educational program." This meant that I had work every day for kids when they came in, and most of them would do it. Monday we did spelling and reading; Tuesday was reading day; Wednesday I gave a spelling pre-test and a composition; Thursday I worked on grammar, usually by correcting Wednesday's essays and reading; and Friday I gave my classes a spelling test and a story to read. My program was highly structured and concentrated on the basics—reading and writing. The kids seemed to like this. They wanted their time structured and seemed to crave regularity, which I gave them. Anytime I gave them choices or opened the period to discussion, it threw my kids into confusion. They became disoriented and immediately started yelling, "What to do Mr. Jones, what to do." This reaction bothered me, because in college I had been a disciple of Summerhill, Kohl, and Holt. I wanted desperately to let the kids find their own materials to work with. It had been my experience that learning became important to me only when I was interested in what I was doing.

As the year progressed, I tried repeatedly to create what Kohl calls the "open classroom." Every attempt I made was a total failure. I asked other teachers about this, and all of them—at least the ones who were doing some teaching—said that I was crazy using "open classroom" techniques on my students. I observed several rooms where I thought teaching was being done, and I found the teachers conducting class just as I did. But one teacher in the faculty room, where I spent most of my periods discussing this problem, told me he had an open classroom and invited me to "share the experience" with him.

I told Portelli about my invitation, and he told me that I was nuts to go because any teacher with an open classroom was either bullshitting or mainlining.

I arrived at Mr. Bloom's classroom before the period started to see how he set up the room. He kept the desks in line and put a bunch of puzzles and games on every other desk. When the bell rang I went to the back of the room to see what would happen. Bloom's door flew open and two kids came in fighting—knocking over a Scrabble game. One of the combatants picked up the Scrabble board and brought it down over his opponent's head. The rest of the kids came running in and began chasing each other around the room. Two or three kids sat down at their desks and began playing, but these games were soon stopped when other kids upset the games or tried to take them over. I had seen enough and began to walk out. Bloom walked over to me and asked my opinion.

"Well, Mr. Bloom, you have a lot of patience."

"Yes, Mr. Jones. You have to if you want to carry this off. I must say that the kids are a bit restless today. Excuse me, Carl is trying to push Jeanette out the window."

Bloom ran to the other side of the room and I left. As I shut the door, a book slammed against it. Was this an "open classroom"? Did playing games teach these kids how to read? Or wasn't that important?

I continued with my own program. There was nothing fancy about it, but at least the kids began to write better and I was comfortable. To break the routine I brought in some books and records, but my kids only became interested in them if I said I was going to give them a grade.

From the very beginning of the year I had marked every paper conscientiously and returned it the next day. I was astonished to find that in other classes most of the kids had never received grades on their papers. When I added comments on them, the kids seemed to appreciate my interest by trying to follow my corrections on their next paper. The handing back of papers became a ritual. Sometimes I was unable to correct all the papers, and the absence of grades the next day affected the initiative of the entire class.

What was happening in my class was the reverse of what I had read about in all my education books. The more I planned, the more I prepared, the more I wrote on papers, the more cooperation and response I received from the class. If I entered the room and told my students they could do whatever they wanted, in their eyes I became like every other teacher in this "raggedy old school." My students seemed to feel that the time I took to prepare dittos and correct papers meant that I cared about them. Discipline improved for me, and I was even able to carry on brief discussion periods with my class. I still had problems, but none that threatened me. If it were not for the administration, the hoodlums roaming the halls, and the few overt behavior problems in my class, I could have done some real teaching. Unfortunately, these ifs made any type of solid education program impossible. I was only one teacher. After my class the kids still had to step out into those ghastly halls, and I still had to review textbooks which in no way met the needs of my students. My kids had to survive, and I had to cover myself. It was a standoff, which meant there could be no continuity, and little progress.

My room became a security blanket for my kids. It was a place where they knew what was going to happen each day and where they could expect to be evaluated for their individual performances. Then the bell would ring, and they would have to go home where there was no certainty, no evaluation, just fear.

I responded to these student reactions by increasing my comments on papers and more carefully planning each period. Every minute of my classroom time was accounted for. When a student finished his work, I always had something else for him to do. Sometimes a student said he was tired of doing work and just sat there. The kids seemed to enjoy these free times immensely and abused them only a few times. After all, they had worked hard for this free time. Why abuse something which was so difficult to earn? That would be like throwing away money after working all day for it. At least that's how my kids saw it.

The room became filled with dittos, textbooks with papers in them, and folders filled with graded papers. My students particularly liked their individual folders because they could look back over their E's and G's (excellent and good). They reviewed their folders regularly, counting the good marks as a miser would count his money. The papers with the longest comments on them were treasured most. At the end of the day I packed everything away in closets to prevent theft and left my room with a feeling of accomplishment, despite the little I was doing to increase my class's reading and writing scores.

Each day I arrived at the school early to run off dittos, if the machine was working. Otherwise I graded papers.

One morning shortly before spring break, as I entered the office to sign in, Simpson came out of his office and gave me a stern look.

"Mr. Jones," Simpson said, "they totaled out your room."

"What do you mean, Mr. Simpson?"

"Why, didn't you hear on the news, Mr. Jones? They tried to burn the school last night, but all they got was your room."

"My room! How much damage is there?"

"Mr. Jones, let's put it this way. You don't have any more room. They burned everything in it. Books, papers, desks. There's just nothing left."

I put my briefcase down and ran out of the office and up the stairs. There was glass and a big puddle of water around the entrance to my room. I opened the door with my key and was met with complete darkness. I switched on the light but no light went on. The windows were boarded up and there were wires hanging from the ceiling. I went over to my closet where the folders were kept, but there was no closet, no desks, just blackness and a foul smell.

I went downstairs again to the room just below mine

and looked out the window onto a pile of rubble with
parts of book covers intermingled with burned desk
tops and crumpled-up folders. There was half a year's
work in that pile. I was disgusted. Who could have
done such a thing? I wondered. Probably some
gangbanger trying to prove he was a man. What a waste.

I went back into the office and into Simpson's room.

"Well, Mr. Simpson, are there any spare rooms in
this school?" Simpson stood up abruptly and leaned
over his desk.

"Mr. Jones, there is no such creature in this school."

"What am I supposed to do with my classes,
Mr. Simpson?"

"Have you spoken to Mr. Barber yet?" Simpson
asked.

"No."

"Mr. Jones, I would suggest that you see him first. He
would know better what room to put you in."

I walked over to the other building where Barber's
office was. He was talking with two policemen when I
arrived. Division was about to begin, so I interrupted to
find out where my class would go.

"Mr. Barber, where should I go with my class for
language arts?"

"Mr. Jones, that's a matter you should take up with
Mr. Simpson. He could tell you better where you
can go."

"Mr. Barber, Mr. Simpson told me that you were the
person who handled such matters."

"Well, Mr. Jones, I don't know why he told you that."

The bell rang and I asked what I should do with
my class.

"Mr. Jones, you just gather your class up and wait

outside in the halls and I'll try to get this thing straightened out."

I managed to collect my class and keep them in line outside the office. Barber came out and handed me a slip of paper with a room number on it.

"Try this one, Mr. Jones."

I walked up three flights of stairs only to find the room occupied. I sent a boy downstairs to Barber to tell him what the situation was. Barber sent me back a note with another number on it.

I proceeded to this room which was on the second floor. It was also occupied. I had my kids run around looking for an empty room and they found nothing. My division was beginning to get restless, and I felt uncomfortable standing out in the hallways, which in the morning were considered free-fire zones.

Barber came puffing up the stairs saying he had been chasing me all over the halls. I told him that so far I was unable to find an empty room.

"Come with me, Mr. Jones. I know where you can go." He led me down the hall to the gym, took out his keys, and opened the door to the balcony overlooking the gym.

"Here you go, Mr. Jones. This will do for the time being."

I was not happy with my new room, if you could call it that, because it was small, hot, and noisy. I also questioned what Barber meant by "time being." For all I knew, that could mean the rest of the year. And most likely that is exactly what it would be. I sat on the edge of the balcony and took attendance. Looking down on the gym class playing basketball, I realized how impossible my attempts to seal out the ghetto environment had been. It was relentless in its pursuit of everyone and everything constructive within the school. Everything it touched it ruined, leaving only despair in its wake. There were no heroes in this school, only victims. I was brought out of my depression by a loud whistle.

I looked down on the gym floor again to see Coach Mills walking across it yelling, "All right, get your black asses out of here and get to class." While he was yelling he was swinging his baseball bat at those kids who didn't move quickly enough. No, I was wrong. There was one hero in this school—the Coach.

11. "You See, All History Is Bullshit."

*M*y preoccupation with planning and grading papers left little time for making friends with members of the faculty. I was not anti-social, just busy. Any relationships I had developed were largely official rather than a matter of personal preference. Yet even the most uninvolved teacher could have sensed an atmosphere of tension among the faculty. No one cared to discuss the problem because its origins were racial, and educated people did not like to admit that such a problem could exist in an "enlightened" environment.

The first overt contact I had with the problem was in my social studies class. I was doing a unit on the newspaper and had been able to get thirty copies of the *Chicago Tribune* free of charge for my class to use. I was not happy using the *Tribune* because of its editorial policy, but at Du Sable you were grateful for any philanthropy which came your way. Besides, the editorials were so often racist that it would make it easier for my kids to understand and criticize them.

Halfway through the unit one of my students in the back of the room asked me why I didn't use the Black Panther newspaper instead of the *Chicago Tribune*. I was stunned by the question because I knew it did not originate in the student's own mind, but had probably been fed to him by someone else.

"Well, Ronald," I answered, "as of now the Black Panthers have not offered thirty issues of their paper for free."

"Mr. Georges says we should throw the *Tribune* back in your face and demand to have the Panther newspaper," Debra yelled.

With that the entire class fell silent as if a great secret had been revealed and they all had been exposed as traitors. The class was waiting for my reaction, and frankly I did not know what to say. I was angry with Georges' unprofessional conduct, and yet I didn't want to lose my cool in front of the class because that was what the kids and Georges would expect. No, I would not publicly criticize anyone until I had investigated the matter and then talked with Simpson.

Tom Georges taught community culture to my social studies class. I didn't know much about him except that every time he sent me a note concerning a discipline problem in my division, there were a lot of spelling mistakes in it. After asking several teachers about the newspaper incident in my class, I found that my experience was not an unusual one. The students in Portelli's class told him that all he was teaching them was white man's history. Portelli reacted as I had, and let the matter pass until he had investigated it further. He told me that the community culture class had been created the year before I arrived to give the kids a knowledge of their community and its problems, as well as possible solutions. In fact the course had become a power base from which the militant black teachers launched their attacks on white teachers. I asked Portelli if Simpson was aware of what Georges was doing.

"Yes," Portelli answered. "Several teachers have gone to Simpson and told him of the situation. But like everyone else in this goddam school, Simpson is scared shitless of anybody who wears an Afro and a dashiki. These militants scare him more than the guys from downtown. All he'd have to do is fire Georges and he'd have every militant and liberal in Chicago down here picketing this hole."

"Couldn't he make formal charges against Georges and let the Board handle it?" I asked.

"Listen, Jones, these are not rational times. That's one thing you have to understand. This town is filled with a bunch of goddam liberals who have nothing better to do than picket and yell obscenities at anyone who disagrees with them. You think those goddam revolutionaries would come to this place and listen to reason. Hell no. They would come down long enough to shake their heads at the terrible conditions, call Simpson a lackey, and then catch a bus to their next demonstration."

"Mr. Portelli, the conditions *are* pretty bad."

"You're goddam right they're bad, but is calling Simpson a lackey or reading the Panther newspaper going to make things any better? Hell no. Let's face it: we're on the firing line. Every day we take our life in our hands coming here and teaching, and all we get for it is abuse from the gangs, the kids, the administration, and now the goddam militants are after our ass. I tell you the shit's getting thicker and this is my last year shoveling it."

I was about to ask Portelli whether he had ever talked with Georges, but he said he needed a cigarette badly and left me for the teachers' lounge. My next stop was the cafeteria, where I found Georges. From what Portelli had said, it would be dangerous to have an open confrontation with him. After all, he was our resident militant and he probably thrived on castrating masochistic white liberals. Better to be subtle at first, I thought, and get the feel of what you're up against.

I was fortunate that the table Georges was sitting at was integrated. I sat down and went through all the formalities of introducing myself, which was a little embarrassing since the school year was half gone and I still did not know anyone at the table. My uneasiness became more bearable when one of the teachers at the table asked me what I was teaching.

"I'm teaching social studies and language arts to Division 204."

"Which subject do you find the most difficult to teach?" he asked me. "So far," I replied, "I think social studies is very difficult to teach. It seems that my students have no sense of time. They have difficulty understanding history because none of it has any relation to the world around them. I noticed Georges' head come up from his plate.

"Yes, I agree with you. These kids have trouble with the basic conceptual framework of history aside from their difficulties with reading the textbook. Tell me, how many hours do you have in history?"

"I had about forty hours in my undergraduate work. I'm going to school now to get my Master's in American intellectual history."

"Well, at least you're better prepared than I am. Why, hell, I was a math major in college, and I'm afraid the kids know I'm unprepared."

"You know, it's funny," Georges interrupted, "but I

98

don't think it's necessary to be prepared well in history. Because, you see, all history, in my opinion, is bullshit."

I was a bit stunned at Georges' remark. Not even my revisionist friends would go as far as saying that all history is bullshit. Obviously the statement was meant to provoke, and I had already committed myself to avoid frontal attacks. I thought it better to ask some questions and see how far Georges would go in defending his axiom. Unfortunately, this course of action proved futile, because Georges gave very little time for questions.

"You see," he continued, "history for the brothers and sisters is a white man's history. Why that Jefferson cat owned some slaves and that Lincoln cat, man, he wanted to send the sisters and the brothers back to Africa. Yet, you see, these men are heroes to white folks." Georges started laughing to himself and repeated the fact that Jefferson had owned slaves.

I tried to interrupt and ask him if he knew what *zeitgeist* meant or to explain to him the danger of taking events out of context. But Georges was rolling now, and I knew that all my training in the discipline of history would not help me in this conversation.

"You see," Georges continued, "our brothers and sisters have been reading propaganda. Yeah, that's the word, man, propaganda. These so-called history books are propaganda, man. Just like in Russia. Only we hide it here, man. You see, all history is class struggle. We got the poor peoples on one side and the rich peoples on the other and, man, you know what goin' to happen. We goin' to have a big war, and the poor people being bigger in the numbers will win, you see. I tell you that all the poor people are colored, and that

99

means the white imperialists will be conquered by the brothers and the sisters, you see. That Marx cat, man, he had something. And Brother Cleaver and the Panthers, man, they read the Marx and got his theory together."

I was about to break in and remind Georges that Marx was white, but, after all, in a monologue that was synthesizing the history of mankind into one lunch period, who could be bothered with such trivialities?

"You see," Georges continued, "when all the poor brothers and sisters find out what those cats at GM are doing to them, then the shit goin' to be bad. They all goin' to grab their jive and bring down the man and end the oppression of the people. Then the people take the power and we get the world together again. You see," Georges started to grin, "this change means revolution, and a lot of fascists are going to die. But that's the price all imperialist cats have to pay for keeping down the people, you see. So I say burn those history books and the people will make their own history. Power is with the people, and we should follow in the steps of Brother Malcolm and Brother Bobby and Sister Angela. Only through picking up the gun against the pigs can the people win."

"Right on," yelled a white teacher with long hair, sitting at the other end of the table. Georges then stood up and exited, leaving us to contemplate the coming revolution. His brief lecture on history convinced me that any rational discussion with him concerning the remarks he made to my class would be futile. I decided that it was time to see Simpson and hope his professional demeanor would be offended by Georges' actions.

100

On my way to Simpson's office I passed Georges' room and decided to see how his bulletin boards looked. If Simpson refused to act on his unprofessional behavior, I could always say that his bulletin boards were poorly done.

The inside of Georges' room was furnished like every other room at Du Sable, except for the many posters hanging from the ceiling and pasted onto the bulletin boards. In front of the room, hanging above his desk, were pictures of Huey Newton, Fred Hampton, and a black woman carrying a baby in one hand and a gun in the other. On the front bulletin board was a picture of Stokely Carmichael and Roy Wilkins. Under Carmichael's picture was written "liberal" and under Wilkins' picture was written "conservative."

In the back of the room, hanging from the ceiling, were pictures of Stokely Carmichael, Malcolm X, and Eldridge Cleaver. On the bulletin board was the beginning of a sentence which read, "We want Land."

I walked over to a table next to Georges' desk which was covered with Panther newspapers and a "Free Angela" poster. Walking out of the room I asked myself, Where does education start and propaganda end? Was it wise to indoctrinate these kids, who, because of their environment, were already prone towards violence, with magazines and posters that openly justified the shooting of policemen? Did the kids really understand and mind what Georges was telling them, or did they assume the same characteristic attitude of indifference towards him as they did about everything else in the school?

My last thought was partially answered by a poster tacked onto Georges' door showing a black mother carrying a naked baby with a gun strapped to the mother's back. On the baby's bottom someone had written with a magic marker, "Kiss my ass."

I had only a few minutes left of my lunch period but decided that something had to be said about Georges' remarks and right away. The office was in a turmoil when I entered because someone had just let the air out of Simpson's tires and he was looking for a gas station to fix them before he left school. I leaned over the counter and asked one of the secretaries whether Simpson was available for a conference; she told me that he was in the vault and to go right in and ask him myself. I walked around the counter, past all the clerks who were looking out the window watching their own cars, and into the vault.

"Mr. Simpson," his back was turned towards me, "would it be possible to have a conference right now?"

Simpson turned around abruptly with the same big grin he always had when he spoke to anyone, even the kids who let the air out of his tires, and replied, "Is it important, Mr. Jones?"

"Yes, Mr. Simpson, it is a very important matter which I feel cannot wait."

"Well, Mr. Jones, if it is that important step into my office and we'll see what the trouble is."

Simpson sat down at his desk and took out his little black notebook and began writing in it. "Now, Mr. Jones," he looked up from his notebook, "what is troubling you?"

"Today in social studies, Mr. Simpson, my students told me that in community culture class Mr. Georges told them that they should throw my *Chicago Tribunes* back in my face and demand to read the Panther newspaper every week. He also told them that I was teaching white man's history and that they should demand that I teach them nothing but black history."

Simpson, who usually wrote in his book when someone talked with him, dropped his pen and just stared at me with eyes that grew larger with every accusation.

"The reason I'm bringing this to your attention, Mr. Simpson, is that I believe this type of conduct is unprofessional. I don't mind Mr. Georges coming to me personally and questioning my qualifications, but when he tells my students to throw papers in my face and demand I teach certain areas, that is another matter which I feel should be dealt with."

Simpson leaned back in his chair. "Mr. Jones, what division told you these things?"

"Division 204," I replied.

He wrote this down in his book.

"Mr. Jones, I think you should understand that some people in this school not only question your qualifications but also mine—so we can all fall victim to such accusations. But I will check into these matters very carefully and then bring it before the Section A Supervisor to see what he says about it. Let me add, Mr. Jones, that we cannot trust everything our students tell us. Anything they tell you about other teachers would be considered hearsay by my superiors. This does not mean that all your accusations are false, merely that it will take a little time to investigate them. Is there anything else, Mr. Jones?"

I shook my head "no" and walked out of the office. Simpson must have sensed that I was disappointed with his response, because he called me back into his office.

"Mr. Jones, I would like to say that I have not been happy with the way Mr. Georges has conducted the community culture class. As you know, it is a new class and one that has no official curriculum. I think this is one of the weaknesses of the program. Why, Mr. Georges hasn't even handed in a plan book yet. I'm not sure what he's doing with his classes."

The bell rang and I excused myself. Walking to my class, I knew nothing was going to be done because Simpson had mentioned taking the matter to District A and that meant that it was too hot for him to handle. The District A Supervisor was white, and he wasn't about to rule on a case involving a black and a white teacher, especially over a question of whether to use the *Chicago Tribune* or the Black Panther newspaper in social studies. If the Supervisor did take action his qualifications might be challenged, and that might mean, God forbid, going back to the classroom. There was no one who had guts enough to challenge Georges, and I would have to accept his provocations if I, as a white, continued teaching in an all-black school. For the first time I began to realize what a black must feel when he is denied justice because of the color of his skin.

12.
The South Dakota Solution

Teaching at Du Sable I found not only that I could keep my class in order, but, more important, at least for my own sanity, that I could go through entire days oblivious to the dangers indigenous to a ghetto school. When I first started teaching at Du Sable all I could think about was my personal safety. Every time I stopped someone in the hall or walked down the stairs I was careful to look over my shoulder or travel with another teacher—preferably Coach Mills. The reason for my extreme caution was obvious to anyone who lives in a big city and reads a daily newspaper. Aside from the rising rate of teacher assaults in ghetto schools or the percentage of increase in crime in ghetto neighborhoods, Du Sable had its own stories of terror which every new teacher heard as part of his unofficial orientation. These stories were not meant to scare you away but to make you aware that the school was not Disneyland, as Feinberg put it. The safety of all teachers, according to the more experienced ones, depended on everyone sticking together, being alert, and knowing when to act and when to retreat. This is why any new teacher had to learn these lessons fast. A weak link in the chain not only endangered that particular teacher but the entire faculty.

As the year progressed I began to forget these early

warnings. In other words, I became cocky. Every incident of assault I tended to blame on the teacher involved. No one, I thought, would get hurt in this school if they were strict enough. My kids would never hit me, much less stab me. I was safe as long as the kids respected me. When I stepped into the hall that was another matter which could be handled by teaming up with another teacher. For me, at least, all those stories at the beginning of the year were either exaggerations or the fault of a teacher who didn't know how to handle the kids.

When I told other teachers my opinion, especially Feinberg, they just stared at me with their mouths open. I began to feel like the weak link they were always talking about. After they finished staring they attacked me with a vehemence I thought was uncalled for considering the subject.

"Listen, Jones," Feinberg yelled at me at lunch one day, "do you know what they did with that 250-pound football coach last month? They pushed him down the stairs and broke his back. Now if those bastards will do that to a gym coach, what the hell do you think they will do with you?"

"Mr. Feinberg," I replied, "was he walking with someone else?"

"Goddammit, Jones, you think that if you follow some of your own safety rules you won't get hurt. If these bastards want to throw you down the stairs, I don't care if you have the 82nd Airborne with you, you're going down those steps head first."

"Leo, don't you think you are exaggerating just a little bit?"

"Goddammit, Jones, don't you realize that these kids

are crazy? They weren't brought up like you and me. When they get pissed at you they don't walk away and curse under their breath. They go and get a gun or knife and kill you, and that's a fact. What you've got to realize, Jones, is that so far you've been lucky. But I'm telling you for your own good, on any given day any given student, even your best ones, could stick a knife in you. If you don't believe that then you've been walking around with your fuckin' eyes shut."

I did not want to continue the argument because Feinberg was getting angrier and more illogical. To calm him down I thought I would get off incidents and onto solutions.

"Well, then, Feinberg," I asked, "what do you propose we all do, walk around with guns and helmets?"

"That isn't such a bad idea," Portelli interrupted. "I wonder if that's legal. Can you imagine, Feinberg, one of those gangbangers walking into your room with his boys and telling you to get fucked, and then you pull out a gun and blow his fuckin' head off?! Shit, you wouldn't have any discipline problems after that."

Feinberg started laughing at Portelli's suggestion, then offered his own solutions. "I think we either all get our asses out of here while they're in one piece, or they put all these bastards on a train and ship them to South Dakota where they all could be put in camps surrounded by barbed wire. Then we would wait until they had all killed each other."

"Leo, that's a better idea than mine. Why don't you submit the idea to Mr. Simpson in a memo?"

"No, Vince," answered Feinberg. "He'd probably think I'm a racist, and he'd get Georges to propagandize my kids and then I'd be in a hell of a mess."

Both Portelli and Feinberg started laughing at each other's suggestions. I didn't pursue the argument, because maybe I had been walking around with my "fuckin' eyes shut." After all, both of these teachers had three years of experience, and maybe I had been lucky so far. When I left the cafeteria some of my self-assurance had dissipated, but it would take more than Portelli's or Feinberg's experiences to change my mind completely.

After mid-term exams I decided to do a unit on the Constitution with my social studies class. I decided not to study the Constitution's origins, philosophy, or content, but rather to concentrate on the first ten amendments and see if the class understood what those rights guaranteed them. This proved to be a good idea. I found that while most of my class had memorized the Bill of Rights in previous social studies classes, they did not really understand how each amendment could be applied to everyday life situations.

The third day of the unit I began discussing search warrants and, specifically, what the Supreme Court considered a legal search. After I explained the meaning of some Supreme Court decisions, the kids proceeded to give me "hypothetical" cases (I found out later that most of these cases were not hypothetical) and waited impatiently for my opinion on how the Court would rule.

I remember this one class very well because it was the only one I had that year that didn't want to leave when the bell rang. When I finally dismissed them, some kids who were outside my room were yelling at the top of their lungs, "Mr. Jones, did you hear the news they just stabbed Mr. Lincoln?"

I grabbed one of the kids by the coat and started asking him questions.

"Listen, Jones," replied the student, "I don't know what happened 'cause the cops made me and Billy come up here. You be the teacher. Go down and find out for yourself."

I let go of the student and started running for the stairs, but I stopped abruptly when I realized what I might find. Was he bleeding badly? My God, was he dead? Suddenly I didn't want to go down those stairs. At the head of the stairwell I could hear police cars and men yelling at kids to clear the hall. My courage returned and I walked down the stairs.

The first floor was a mass of confusion. By the office door a plain-clothes policeman with his gun drawn was holding a woman against the wall. There was a trail of blood coming from the library and leading into the office. Feinberg was standing by the gym door with his window pole trying to get students to go to their classes. I walked over to him just as the ambulance attendants entered the building.

"What the hell happened, Feinberg?" I asked.

"They really did a number on Lincoln."

"Who did?"

"Lincoln threw some kid out of his room and the kid went home and got his mother and she came down and started to fight with Lincoln and then she stabbed him. From what I hear the kid and his brother helped the old woman out. Wish the hell they had that train ready for South Dakota. Those bastards would be the first ones on it."

I walked around the corner to Lincoln's room. There was a trail of blood right up to his front door. Lincoln

was the tall black teacher who at the beginning of the
year had complained about the security in the building.
Shit, why didn't the administration ever listen to
teachers? Well, there would be no way for Simpson to
cover this up. I turned around to go back to the office
to see how Lincoln was.

On my way back I was met by Simpson and Barber.
Both men looked agitated and were visibly upset when
they saw the blood on the floor.

"Mr. Jones," yelled Simpson from the library, "has
the janitor arrived yet?"

I shook my head no. Simpson turned to Barber.

"I want a janitor here immediately to clean this up,
and tell him to start in the office first." Barber left
immediately. Simpson just stood there looking at the
blood as if it were a poorly done bulletin board.

When I arrived at the office, Lincoln had not been
removed yet. He was filling out an accident report—a
Board of Education rule. Lincoln probably thought it
best to fill out the report now rather than wait for a
memo from Simpson on his failure to comply with
Board policy. It seemed the Board had a form for every
occasion, even a stabbing. Simpson came back from
the scene of the crime and asked all the teachers who
saw what happened to write up a report in duplicate.
Feinberg was still standing by the gym entrance
shaking his head.

"What's wrong, Feinberg?" I asked.

"Shit, Jones, look at those fools in there. Some
bastards just stabbed a teacher and all they're worrying
about is the blood on the floor and that goddam accident
report. If I were Lincoln I would stand up and bleed
all over the sons of bitches. You know what the real

shame is, Jones? They'll probably give the bastard who stabbed him probation because he's socially deprived. Then after they free the bastard they'll blame Lincoln for the stabbing because his bulletin board didn't motivate or his lesson plans didn't follow the proper format. This fuckin' school is a disgrace."

Feinberg and I walked silently back to the library. The janitors had arrived and were busy cleaning up the blood. I could hear a substitute teacher in Lincoln's room trying to quiet down the kids so he could continue with Lincoln's program, which could not be interrupted under any circumstances. I sat down with Feinberg in the back of the library and we just looked at each other. We didn't say anything because everything that needed to be said had been said already. Both of us knew that nothing would come of this incident. There would be an investigation by the police and the Board. They would make recommendations, and Simpson would inform us of them through a memo, and that would end the matter. If someone else got stabbed, Simpson would show the people uptown the memo he had distributed after the first stabbing, and then they would shake their head in approval and write up a memo on Simpson's memo. In the meantime, while they were all shaking their heads, we were told to get our plan books in on time and to make sure our bulletin boards were student-oriented.

My thoughts were interrupted by a student who stuck his head in the door. He was wearing a big leather hat and carrying a stick in his hand.

"Hey, man," asked the student, "you got any scissors lying around?"

"Which teacher needs them?" I asked.

"No teacher needs them. I needs them."

"What do you need them for?"

"Man, I wants to gets me another teacher like they got Lincoln." The kid started laughing and ducked out of the room. I looked back at Feinberg who now had his head in his hands.

"Feinberg," I asked, "what time does that train leave for South Dakota?"

B. Mutiny

*T*he stabbing of Lincoln shook up the entire faculty. Teachers began traveling in pairs and made sure no one was behind them when they started a lesson or were walking in the hallway. When parents came to school they were asked to stay in the office until the teacher was free to see them.

The administration reacted to the incident typically, by sending out a flood of memos reminding the teachers of school security procedures and the importance of good planning in deterring violence in the classroom. The following are random samples of the memos I received after the stabbing:

SAFETY

Windows should be opened from the top or six inches from the bottom. Dangerous situations develop when this regulation is not observed by teachers.

STUDENT TOYS

Teachers please advise your students not to bring toys such as klackers, basketballs, bats and balls.

TOYS AND FOOD

Teachers and aides are to enforce regulations that balls, klackers and food are not allowed in the building.

ASSAULTS

All assaults, whether verbal or physical, should be reported to the office at once.

LESSON PLAN BOOKS

Lesson plan books of ALL teachers are due in the main office each Tuesday by 8:24 A.M. Teachers absent on that day must submit plans upon return.

EIGHTH-GRADE TEACHERS

All eighth-grade teachers are reminded to please check their mailboxes frequently in Room 101.

THE ILLINOIS CONSTITUTION AND FLAG ETIQUETTE

Student copies of the Illinois Constitution and Flag Etiquette still have not been picked up from office #101 in too many instances. How are these documents being taught, if at all?

REMINDER—FIRE DRILLS AND ALARMS

Teachers and Teacher Aides are again reminded that ALL personnel must leave the building in the event of a fire drill or alarm.

More memos came during my class periods, instructing me what to do in certain situations and reminding me to keep my records in order, especially those for attendance. None of these attempts at calming the faculty was successful. Most of us were damn scared now and just waiting for the next incident. We all knew that good plans, beautiful bulletin boards, or even being black didn't make a bit of difference when a student went nuts. If you got in the way of that kid, you were going to get hurt. Some teachers, particularly the militants, tried to act as if the incident were Lincoln's fault and something that could never happen to them because they related so well; but the rest of the faculty thought different.

We had not yet received our first report on Lincoln's recovery when some students from the high school threw a desk at one of the women teachers on the second floor and then pulled a knife on her. I found out about the assault at the end of the day and spent that night preparing a speech for Simpson demanding that he get some security for the school or close it down. When I walked into the building the next day I found that most of the teachers had prepared similar speeches, and it looked to me like Simpson had a full-grown mutiny on his hands.

The day went by uneventfully. Most of the teachers vented their anger in little groups during free periods, or on hall duty posts. I was fed up with all this talk and decided something dramatic had to be done and done right away before everyone calmed down over the incident. I told Feinberg of my disgust and asked him what action the teachers as a group could take to make the administration aware of their feelings. Feinberg listened to me and kept nodding in agreement. He put down his window pole and took me out into the hall.

"You know, Jones, you're right. There is just too much goddam talk in this hole. My Dad's a union man, and when he gets screwed by management he calls over the union steward and they shut the goddam place down until the matter's straightened out. But not teachers. They get degrees and think that all their troubles can be talked over and straightened out in a gentlemanly fashion. Goddammit if we don't get shit on every time. I think you're right. It's time this faculty stopped talking and got their hands dirty. That's the only thing administrations understand. Let's go upstairs and see how many teachers have guts enough to walk out of this place. Let Simpson get off his ass and come over here and motivate."

Both of us ran upstairs and started knocking on doors. Surprisingly, only three teachers were unwilling to walk out. We all gathered in the hall and decided to sign out immediately without offering any explanations. We began walking to the head of the stairs when a teacher's aide met us with a memo from Simpson. The memo instructed all teachers to dismiss their students early so that teachers would be able to participate in an in-service meeting that afternoon.

After reading the memo, the group decided to hear what Simpson had to say and postpone any action until after the meeting. Most of the teachers in our group already saw this meeting as a victory, but I, along with Feinberg, felt that it was an administrative ploy and that nothing of any worth would come of it. What disappointed me most about the memo was its impact on our little group's solidarity. Not five minutes before the memo was read there were twelve teachers in that hallway ready to walk out. Now everyone was returning to his classroom and saying that "Simpson isn't such a bad guy." What a letdown. I looked for Feinberg and saw him enter Portelli's room.

He came out of the room just as I entered, and said to me, "What did I tell you, Jones? All teachers are chickenshits."

When I arrived at the room where the in-service meeting was to be held, only a few teachers were huddled in the back, waving their hands frantically at each other. I hoped that the apparent intensity of their discussion would characterize the teachers' response when the meeting got under way. I was sick of always shaking my head in agreement when Simpson said something, then complaining afterward to Feinberg about his decision. Feinberg never rebuked me for my cowardice because he felt that when you talked to an administrator it was best to agree with him no matter what he said—and then go ahead and do what you wanted to in the first place. True, this was the wisest procedure to follow in any confrontation with the office; but the issue at hand demanded a strong administrative reaction immediately, before the kids got the idea that all the teachers had to back them up was a discipline card and a bulletin board. There was no way to avoid a confrontation on this issue.

Simpson's late entrance went unnoticed because all the teachers were busy talking in small groups. I could hardly wait for his opening remark.

"Good afternoon, teachers. I called this meeting because in view of recent events I thought maybe we should take a look at our program of instruction and see if it's meeting our students' needs. So I have asked the heads of our departments to set up an in-service in each subject area, and hopefully this will give a boost to our students."

I couldn't believe it. How could a man be that insensitive to what was going on in the hallways and classrooms? Did he really believe that an in-service meeting would prevent stabbings? No one said a word. Probably they were just as shocked as I was at Simpson's opening comments and didn't know how to start to complain. Everything seemed so obvious. I didn't want to say anything, but suddenly my hand was in the air and Simpson looked to the side and recognized me.

"Yes, Mr. Jones."

"Mr. Simpson, aren't we going to talk about Mr. Lincoln?" I heard a murmur in the back of the room and teachers shifting in their chairs. Simpson turned from me and faced the faculty again.

"How many teachers feel that we should discuss the recent attacks on two of our staff?"

Someone yelled from the back, "We better discuss it now or no one is coming back to this place."

"Perhaps our time," Simpson continued, "would be better spent if we broke up into buzz groups and discussed the problem and possible solutions, rather than carry through with our scheduled in-service."

Simpson distributed different colored construction paper to each of us. We were to form groups according to the color paper we received. Although Feinberg and Portelli received different color paper than mine, we all decided to sit together. It was time for action, and none of us wanted to get stuck in a group that would just recommend a committee to study the root causes of the assaults.

Our group was larger than the others because of the addition of Feinberg and Portelli. I was especially pleased to see Coach Mills with us, and I wished secretly that we had the guts to nominate him for principal as one of our recommendations. We also had the woman teacher who had been attacked on the second floor, and a special reading assistant who had become a legend when she called Barber an "overgrown gorilla" to his face. I was satisfied that even if the groups produced nothing, at least there would be some colorful exchanges in our meeting.

The young teacher from the second floor began by asking us if we thought we should have a recording secretary. We all nodded, except for Coach Mills.

"Shit, man," the coach explained. "I don't give a damn if you take notes, but I wouldn't want anyone quoting me directly, if you know what I mean."

All of us snickered, except the woman from the second floor who just looked confused.

"I think what the coach is trying to say," Portelli interrupted, "is that none of us should be quoted but rather all recommendations should be presented as a group consensus."

"Exactly," Feinberg continued. "That way they can't pick out individuals to ridicule or question. All of us know damn well what the situation is. This is no time to start arguing with Simpson over bulletin boards or plan books. We need to get right to the issue, stay on it, formulate a solution, and stick to it until Simpson either accepts it or kicks us all out of here."

"Amen, Brother," said the reading teacher.

"Well, Mr. Feinberg. What do you propose as a solution?" asked the young teacher from the second floor.

"I think the first thing we need in this school is some police who aren't afraid of kicking some ass. This place is up for grabs, and we can't do anything until there is some order."

"Isn't that a little drastic, Mr. Feinberg?" replied the young teacher.

Feinberg's face turned red. He started moving his lips

123

but nothing came out. The silence was broken by the coach.

"Shit, man. Some dudes threw a desk at you and threatened you with a blade. Last week Mr. Lincoln was stabbed several times. Don't you think that's a little drastic?"

Feinberg regained his composure just as the Coach finished.

"Goddammit. What the hell do you liberals need to convince you? Does someone have to get killed before you realize what you're up against?"

"Amen, Brother," said the special reading teacher.

"I think we ought to call all the students together and rap with them," suggested the young teacher.

"I'll rap the little bastards," said the Coach. "Right in their goddam peanut brains."

"That's the trouble, Mr. Mills," retorted the young teacher. "These kids have been hit too much."

Now the Coach became speechless. He kept moving his lips but nothing came out. The special reading assistant who was seated next to the Coach leaned over and put her hand on his lap.

"Before the Coach goes on I would like to say something about the kids we are dealing with. I was brought up in this neighborhood and managed with a lot of luck to get out of it. Now despite what the professors say and the militants yell, this ghetto environment is just plain bad for any kid. Unless you are strong and have parents who are strong, the street is going to beat you. So we are dealing with kids who are tough. They only respect superior force. You can't reason with them because their reasoning is so much different than ours. We can't talk to them about going to college or what it means not to have a good education. They just don't understand that kind of talk because there is nothing in their everyday life that illustrates what we are telling them. The only thing they see is pimps riding around in Cadillacs, and gang members taking their parents' money and living high on it. Until these kids can live in an area where education is held in high esteem, and they can see people of their own race get jobs because of that education, you can't start rapping with them. Unfortunately, our country has not made that commitment yet, and that leaves us in a pretty bad situation."

"What do you mean by a bad situation?" asked the young teacher from the second floor.

"I mean that all the teachers at Du Sable are caught in the middle. The kids think that all education is bullshit. They can't see any value in it right now. Because of this, they have no respect for teachers or what we are trying to do. The administration and the Board of Education, in order to justify their existence, must explain why the kids do so poorly on their reading tests, so they blame the person who has the most contact with the kids—us. The teachers are stuck in overcrowded classrooms without any facilities or training in remedial education, and they're expected to raise the kids' reading scores by three or four years. What really happens is that the teacher finds himself being attacked by the kids in the classroom, and when he seeks help from the administration they attack him for poor bulletin boards or poor planning."

The special reading teacher sat back in her chair after she finished. Her presentation of the problem was so thorough and succinct that no one spoke—there wasn't anything one could add, or for that matter, criticize. I was amazed at her composure, considering the events of the past week.

"Miss Florence," I said, "I think your presentation of the problem is correct. Now what do you propose as a solution?"

"Well, Mr. Jones," she started to smile, "I have to agree with Mr. Feinberg. This school is a disgrace. I think we have to be realistic and accept the fact that we are not going to educate the majority of the kids in this school. But I do think there are some kids in this school who have potential and could make it with our help if we didn't have to contend with all the others and the trouble they cause. I don't mean to suggest that we dispense with all the dumb kids, just the ones who are causing severe disturbances. We could start helping those few good kids by first making them feel safe in their learning environment; and, second, by setting up standards of conduct and achievement which will restore some legitimacy to the school's educational program. But I would like to add that these are only stop-gap measures which can only temporarily help our position. I believe ultimately that the system of education in Chicago will cease to function unless somebody or some group in power makes some drastic decisions right now concerning not only black people's education but also their housing and job opportunities. I think that all we teachers can do now is focus on our own safety and maybe help some kids in the process."

"I move we accept Miss Florence's proposal to focus on teacher and student safety as the main priority in our school," said Portelli. "All those in favor raise their hands."

Everyone in the group raised his hand with the exception of the Coach, who was awakened from a deep daze by the vote.

"Just exactly what are we going to say to Simpson when we break up?" Portelli asked.

Before any of us could answer, Simpson announced that time was running out and that we should all return to the general meeting to discuss our results. Feinberg stood up abruptly and told the group he would present Miss Florence's proposal to the general meeting if it was all right with the rest of us. We all nodded in agreement and moved our chairs back into position. Simpson, who had been circulating around the room listening in on different groups, was sitting on the desk in front of the room.

"I hope," Simpson began, "that these buzz groups have proved to be a rewarding experience. Now, with the little time we have left, I think we should share our experiences with the entire group."

"Mr. Simpson," yelled Mr. Clips from the back of the room, "before we start I, along with the entire faculty, would like to thank you for letting us get together in this manner to discuss some of the pressing problems which are facing our school. I have been here for ten years and sincerely believe that we can make this place work despite what has happened in recent weeks."

I could hear teachers twisting in their chairs. It seemed that every time Du Sable had a crisis, Clips felt it his obligation, no matter what the issues were, to give his "We can make this place work" speech. From the movement in the room and the murmur of voices, I suspected that most teachers were fed up with it.

Clips was still going on about the traditions of Du Sable when I heard Feinberg whisper, "Enough of this bullshit." He stood up and addressed the meeting.

"I don't mean to cut you off, Mr. Clips," Feinberg said. "But since time is so limited I want to present to Mr. Simpson the proposals we formulated in our group."

"That's quite all right," Clips replied, "I often get carried away talking about Du Sable and you will all have to excuse me, but I'm sure all of you know how I feel about this school."

I thought he was going to start up again, but he sat down when Feinberg turned his head and motioned something at him.

"Briefly," Feinberg continued, "our group decided that the teachers in this school are all in immediate danger of physical assault, whether it be from outside people or pupils in our charge. We discussed the causes of this danger and decided that the best course of action is to ask for more security police in this school. Our group feels the situation at Du Sable cannot be handled effectively by administrative personnel or by teachers; it needs professional attention. We feel that the priority right now should be the protection of the staff and students."

Feinberg started to say something else, but Georges jumped up and cut him off.

"You see, Mr. Simpson, what we have here is a plan for the repression of our brothers and sisters. You can't blame the kids for what is happening, you see, but all of society. Do I make myself clear? The action I propose is to get at the root causes of the problem. Only by getting at the roots can we solve the problem."

"I disagree," Feinberg was still standing, "with Mr. Georges' proposal because we as teachers cannot be expected to change much less identify the many causes that have made this school a jungle. The President, the Congress, the Supreme Court, the intellectuals, and a hell of a lot of money have all failed to ameliorate the conditions that make this school an impotent institution. So I cannot understand how a classroom teacher can be expected to get at the root causes. I think our only alternative is to try to protect ourselves and do the best we can in the classroom."

Some teachers in the back of the room began to applaud. Clips and Georges jumped up at the same time, asking for permission to speak to the group. Simpson's characteristic smile turned into a determined frown, which he always wore when there were disagreements among his faculty. Disagreements meant Simpson had to make decisions, and God knows how he hated to do that, especially on an issue as inflammatory as bringing the police into a ghetto school. He probably was thinking what a fool he had been to offer the idea of buzz groups in the first place. That would be the last time he would use any of those fancy textbook ideas. Clips and Georges were still talking in unison when Simpson stood up and waved his hands as if he were a magician trying to make all of us disappear. Clips and Georges sat down in response to Simpson's gestures.

"I'm sorry to cut you off, Mr. Clips and Mr. Georges, but time has run out."

After Simpson said this, he just stared at us without

saying a word. I got the feeling that he had looked at his watch and mechanically announced the end of the meeting without realizing that no solutions had been reached. Unfortunately for Simpson, he became aware of this fact in the middle of his announcement and now was stuck for something to say. The silence, which was becoming embarrassing to everyone in the room, amused me because it was the first time I had seen Simpson, the perfect administrator, speechless. The silence would continue until Simpson discovered that none of his pat answers fit the current problem, which meant he had to think up something original. Consequently we all sat there hoping his cognitive processes weren't as limited as all of us thought.

"The debate which we have all been listening to has been, in my opinion, very instructive."

Simpson was stalling, and we all knew it.

"I have learned from the conversation that teachers can in open discussion iron out their difficulties. Hopefully, these gatherings will help us improve our instructional program. There have been several proposals made here and all of them have merit. The question is: Which one will benefit the children and our institution the most?"

All the teachers began moving in their seats and whispering. If Simpson didn't stop beating around the bush he would be responsible for the ensuing fist fight between Georges and Feinberg, who were already standing up.

"I have decided that you, the teachers, should make the decision rather than I. Tomorrow I will call the Wentworth police district captain and ask him to send down a representative to tell us how they handle

130

security in a school such as Du Sable. After the representative puts his case on the table, you, the staff, will vote whether to have the security or to continue without it. I personally feel that we don't need any help here at Du Sable. I admit there have been some incidents which speak to the contrary, but I think Du Sable is a dynamic place and can adjust to these interruptions in our educational program. You are dismissed for tonight. We will all meet back here tomorrow morning."

Simpson had to be commended for his quick thinking. I didn't think he would come up with something. He had covered himself by letting us all know that he didn't think we needed police in this place. When news of this got downtown and to the community, he would be commended for his stand against police and repression and for dynamic education. In the end, the teachers would be blamed for the tightened security.

14. Sergeant Jackson

The next morning I arrived early as always to run off some dittos. Despite the early hour, the meeting room was filled with teachers in little groups discussing the upcoming police presentation. After I finished with my work, I went into the room and sat with the group I had been with the day before.

I could tell from listening to the various gatherings around me that this meeting would not reach consensus. Georges was yelling "Off the pig" on the other side of the room, while Coach Mills was asking me, if he made a citizen's arrest, would that be considered police brutality? Simpson walked into the room alone, and from the looks of most teachers they were disappointed. Simpson had tricked us again. I made up my mind that if he tried to bullshit his way out of this, I was getting the hell out of this place.

"Good morning, teachers," Simpson began. "After the meeting yesterday, I called the Wentworth police station and asked them whether it would be possible to have a policeman come down here and discuss with us how they secure a school. I was informed by the district captain that he has under him a task force which is specifically designed to secure schools that are having trouble with their student bodies. This task force is made up of plain-clothes policemen who have training in riot control and, most important, in my opinion, community relations."

"We want ass-kickers, not do-gooders," grumbled the Coach under his breath.

Simpson looked at his watch and then looked up at us with a blank face.

"I'm sorry for this delay, teachers, but the captain told me that the head of the task force, Sergeant Jackson, would be here at nine-thirty."

"If I were Jackson," whispered Feinberg "and knew where they were sending me, I wouldn't even show up."

The room remained silent except for Georges, who was saying something about Algeria when a short, stocky, black man with a limp came into the room. He had a scar across his cheek and he looked awful "bad," as my kids would say. He just stood in the corner and said nothing. Simpson turned his head and motioned the man to come over to the desk.

"Teachers, I would like to introduce to you Sergeant Jackson, who will tell you exactly what his task force does and the successes they have had. Sergeant Jackson."

Sergeant Jackson just stared at us and said nothing. He looked embarrassed, as if this were the first time he had ever been in front of a group. He finally put his hands on his hips, revealing a large gun, and began to talk in a low, gravelly voice.

"I'm not too sure what Mr. Simpson or you teachers want to hear. All I can tell you is that many schools in Chicago have had trouble with their school bodies. This trouble can either be a riot or an increase in teacher assaults, or anything that involves consistent criminal activities in and around school property. Our task force was set up to go into a troubled school and quiet it down without causing any friction with the community. That's why we don't wear uniforms. So far we have been pretty successful. It took us a week to clean up Lane Tech and about two weeks at South Shore High School. We must have done a good job, because not one of these schools has called us back. Are there any questions?"

Jackson said this last sentence with a smile which brought some warmth to his face. Georges raised his hand and was recognized by Jackson.

"Sergeant Jackson, could you tell us exactly what you mean by cleaning up a school?"

"Well, first we tell the principal that all kids have to have passes to be in the halls. Then we question anyone who doesn't have a pass. If this person is trespassing, we arrest him. If we catch a kid vandalizing or shooting dope, we pick him up. Does that answer your question?"

"No, not quite," Georges replied. "What do you do if the student refuses to go?"

Jackson smiled again. "Well, that doesn't happen too often."

"I'll bet it doesn't happen too often," Portelli whispered.

"Sergeant Jackson," yelled Feinberg, "if a student is by his locker and I tell him to move and he tells me to get fucked, will you step in?"

"Yes, if you asked me to I would go over to the boy and tell him to move."

"What if he didn't?"

Jackson looked confused by that comeback.

"Listen, I don't know what you're getting at, but if I go over to a locker and ask a boy to move and he doesn't move, then he's going to end up in the hospital."

Virtually everyone in the room began applauding wildly after Jackson's comment. Feinberg was jumping up and down in his chair yelling "Jackson for principal" at the top of his lungs.

Simpson came out of the corner and took charge of the meeting again. As Sergeant Jackson was leaving the room, he turned and addressed us after excusing himself to Simpson.

"One thing I must tell you teachers and Mr. Simpson. The only way we can come into a school and be effective is if we are given a free hand. We cannot do our job properly if the principal or the faculty interfere. My men will not act until this faculty gives them the complete go-ahead. When you do that, then we will proceed to apprehend and stop any criminal actions in this school. I think it is only fair to tell you that we have been most effective in schools that have a good discipline procedure. Our job is limited to criminal violations. We will be glad to help teachers and administrators in apprehending violators of school policy, but the punishment of these violators will have to rest with school authorities. If your discipline procedure is effective in dealing with the people we bring in, then your school has a good chance of remaining secure after we leave. If there aren't any questions, I will let you discuss the matter with Mr. Simpson. Thank you for allowing me to come down and explain our procedures."

Sergeant Jackson's final comments were disappointing to me because Du Sable didn't have any discipline procedure—which meant that when the task force left, all hell would break loose. I guess I would have to be satisfied to see some kids disciplined for a week. Simpson had resumed his position at the front of the room, and Georges was already on his feet.

"Mr. Simpson, may I make some comments concerning Sergeant Jackson's presentation?"

"Certainly, Mr. Georges," replied Simpson.

"Mr. Simpson, I would like to protest this obvious attempt at oppressing the brothers and the sisters. You see, all history is a record of oppression of black people, and you are perpetuating this oppression, you see."

I thought all history was bullshit, but I guess all history, to Georges, was a number of things depending on the situation. Simpson looked perplexed after Georges sat down. Then he laid the bombshell.

"Mr. Georges, I cannot see how your talk of oppression is relevant to the current situation."

Georges leaped to his feet along with four other teachers wearing Afros and dashikis. Simpson picked a fine time to put his foot in his mouth.

"You see," Georges shouted, waving his fist, "most of the teachers in this room are going to use the police to get discipline in their classes. If they have trouble with a kid, you see, they will send him out in the hall without a pass and then let the pigs beat him up."

Feinberg jumped up along with Portolli. I thought the entire faculty was going to witness a tag-team wrestling match if Simpson didn't step in and mediate the debate. Simpson looked like he was still trying to figure out what he had said that had offended Georges. He motioned to Feinberg and Portelli to sit down, which they did. Georges was still on his feet, but he wasn't saying anything. The entire room fell silent.

Whatever Simpson had to say, it better be good.

"Teachers, before I comment on the debate, I want to hear from Mr. McCready who has had his hand up for the last ten minutes."

McCready was our EMH teacher. He was friendly and worked hard at his job. Most EMH teachers I knew in Chicago just went into their rooms with a baseball bat and crayons, hoping that everyone in the class would cut. But McCready took his job seriously.

I enjoyed talking to him because he had a quiet and appealing wisdom about him. When I first met him and found out he was teaching EMH, I told him he had gotten screwed. "You better see Simpson immediately about getting a transfer, Mr. McCready," I suggested.

McCready just smiled at me and replied, "Mr. Jones, aren't all the kids in this school EMH? The only difference between my classes and your classes is that I have seven kids and you have thirty. No, Mr. Jones, you're the one that's getting screwed."

When my room was burned out I was really depressed and spent most of the day sulking in the faculty room feeling sorry for myself. McCready came over to me during his lunch break and asked me what was lost in the fire. I recounted about ten items while he stood there shaking his head in sympathy. After I finished, he leaned over and whispered in my ear, "If you want my opinion about the whole thing, Mr. Jones, these niggers aren't worth shit around here."

It was the same McCready to whom Simpson gave the privilege of the final statement.

"Mr. Simpson," McCready was getting to his feet, "I haven't been following the debate too closely, so I have no comment on that. But I do have a question to ask."

"Go ahead, Mr. McCready."

"I don't know what Board of Education rules are, but if we don't get the police in here, would it be legal for the teachers in the school to carry a gun?"

The faculty burst out laughing. Simpson began to smile for the first time since Lincoln was stabbed.

"Well, Mr. McCready," said Simpson smiling, "I'm not sure what the Board says about teachers carrying firearms in the school."

"I wish you would find out, Mr. Simpson," retorted McCready, "because if those police don't come into this school, I'm going to get me a gun and protect myself."

"Thank you, Mr. McCready, for your comments. Teachers, I frankly don't think we need police in this building. But since some of you have expressed a different opinion, I have decided to take a vote. Whatever the majority rules, I will carry out."

Simpson was cleverer than I thought. The situation definitely did not lend itself to administrative fiat. He had to pass the buck somehow, and since no one there was higher in rank than he, the responsibility had to be passed to the faculty.

"All those in favor of *not* having Sergeant Jackson's task force come into Du Sable, raise their hands."

Three people put their hands up. You could feel an electricity go through the faculty.

"All those in favor of having Sergeant Jackson's task force come into Du Sable, raise their hands." The room was filled with waving.

Feinberg started yelling, "We did it, we did it."

Simpson was still counting. This had to be official in case he was called downtown.

"Our time is gone, teachers," Simpson yelled over

the cheering. "I will tell Sergeant Jackson that he may secure the school, and there will be no strings attached."

I got up to leave when I heard Feinberg say to Portelli, "You two-faced bastard. How come you didn't vote to have the cops come in? Are you trying to get some pull with Simpson?"

I turned around to see how Portelli would get out of his obvious betrayal.

"Hell yes, I voted to keep those cops out. As it stands now, McCready won't bring his gun in."

"Shit," said Feinberg, "let's have a re-vote."

15.

Walkout

hile Sergeant Jackson was kicking the
hoodlums out of school, the militants decided that they
needed a new approach to fight the white imperialist
pigs who were invading their school with cops. The
dilemma facing the militants was whom to attack and
what weapons to use.

They weren't about to go after Sergeant Jackson
because he would punch them in the mouth and make
an arrest. He was a pig, and a tough pig at that. Best
leave him alone. Simpson was another useless target.
His vacillations in the last week would have made
the diplomats at Munich blush. No matter what the
militants did to Simpson, he wouldn't take a stand. They
had to have someone, preferably white, who would
stand up for his principles; they could then cover him
with black rhetoric until he either surrendered
peacefully or became so enraged that he did something
stupid, such as hitting one of them. If an assault
occurred, the militants would go into the brutality rap
and the man's career in teaching would be ended. The
publicity they would get from the incident would
establish the militants as the new leaders of the
community—which was nothing to sneeze at, especially
in liberal circles.

But for the time being, to find such a person or group

143

of persons would have to wait. Better to get an issue, then choose the victim. Finding the issue was much easier: Du Sable was a gold mine. Even the dumbest radical could find something to complain about within minutes after entering the school. In fact, Du Sable was so bad that you couldn't pick out just one grievance but needed a list, which is just what the militants submitted.

One more item was needed to make this a true demonstration—a vehicle to carry it out. This last qualification was easier to find than a grievance. Du Sable had 850 kids who hated everything and anything connected with the school. All they needed was a little guidance and the rest could be ad libbed. And, boy, could they ad lib.

I, along with most of my colleagues, was not aware of what was going on until one morning I found a mimeographed sheet in my mailbox which read:

Concerned Students of Du Sable Demand:
1. More black teachers
2. Reinstatement of Mr. Rivers, the music teacher
3. Better organized school
4. Black and qualified principal
5. New lunch room and gym

Funny they weren't demanding better bulletin boards. On the bottom of the sheet was written an ultimatum: "Either these demands be discussed with the administration before noon or a walkout will take place at 2:30 this afternoon."

Feinberg, who had the mailbox next to me, slapped me on the back and started yelling at the top of his lungs, "The little bastards are walking out. Did

144

you read the bottom? The little bastards are walking out. . . ."

Feinberg was yelling so loud that Simpson came out of his office. Frankly, I was a little embarrassed. "Little bastards" wasn't the correct pedagogic term for our student body, and Simpson demanded preciseness above all else at Du Sable. Simpson called Feinberg over to the main desk. Feinberg said nothing, he simply handed Simpson the ditto with a big smile on his face, as if Simpson, too, would start yelling, "Hey, staff, the little bastards are walking out." But Simpson was too professional for that. He read the ditto, walked into his office, and returned with a sign which he attached to the main desk bulletin board. It read:

TO: All Staff Members
FROM: Mr. Simpson, Acting Principal
RE: Walkout

All staff members will be expected to carry out a normal program throughout the entire day, Oct. 21, 1970. There will be a brief faculty meeting at 8:24 in Room 179.

Thank you.

R. Simpson

After reading the memo, I started for Room 179. Portelli came with me. He was still reading the circular.

"Well, Jones, after four months of fucking us over, the kids finally decided to get Simpson."

"What do you mean, Portelli?"

"Jones, when word of this walkout gets downtown or, heaven forbid, if some newspaper gets hold of it, Simpson will be lucky if he gets a job as a janitor in this school system."

145

"You mean they'd hold something like this against Simpson?"

"Jones, where the hell have you been?" Portelli yelled. "Don't you know by now that the Board only wants Simpson to do one goddam thing at Du Sable, and that's to keep this hole quiet? When these bastards start walking out, every goddam liberal in the city will be down here with signs, cameras, experts, and God knows what else to crucify somebody."

"You can't blame Simpson for this mess."

"Exactly, Jones, and after they start questioning Simpson it won't take those softheaded liberals too long to find out who is really to blame. One thing the Board doesn't like is people who make waves. This walkout, in my opinion, looks like one hell of a disturbance."

"Mr. Portelli, do you really think the Board would transfer Simpson out of here?"

"Jones, look around you. Doesn't it seem strange to you that all the teachers at Du Sable are either very young or very old?"

"No, it hasn't, Portelli. But so what?"

"Jones, don't you get it? Du Sable is a dumping ground for new teachers and for older radicals who made waves on the north side. If you fuck up in a good school in Chicago, or need a job desperately, they put you in a school like Du Sable where you either get killed or are too busy staying alive to make any waves. Now, if you manage to fuck up here you're in trouble. Shit, they might make Simpson a visiting teacher in one of those projects, and I don't have to tell you what that means."

Portelli was still going on about where they might send Simpson when Barber called the meeting to order.

I wondered where Simpson was. If Portelli was right, he probably was looking in the want ads.

"Good morning, teachers," Barber began. "Mr. Simpson will be with us in just a moment. Meanwhile, I would like to acquaint you with the various emergency bells we have at Du Sable so you will know what to do in case of an emergency."

For the first time at Du Sable I began to get really scared. I couldn't believe a dittoed note could cause this much panic.

"When you hear a bell with a gong-gong sound, that is the fire alarm. You should usher your kids out of the room as quickly as possible, following the routes mapped out in your Du Sable Teacher's Handbook. If you hear a long bell with no gong-gong sound, that is the air-raid signal, which means you should bring your students to the basement immediately."

"And pray to God," said Feinberg in a hoarse, loud voice, "that those Reds make a direct hit."

"What was that, Mr. Feinberg?"

"Nothing, Mr. Barber," answered Feinberg.

"Finally," Barber went on, "a short bell sound followed by silence means that some type of emergency exists in the school. All teachers should be sure that their classroom doors are locked and their students are quiet. Are there any questions?"

Mr. Lincoln, who had just returned from the hospital, raised his hand and was recognized by Barber.

"Mr. Barber, I'm not quite clear on just what constitutes an emergency inside the school."

Barber looked a bit perturbed, as though he didn't wish to spell it out.

"Mr. Lincoln," cut in Mr. Daniels, "remember when

147

the Stones came running through the halls last year shooting at each other?"

Lincoln shook his head in agreement.

"Well, that's what they mean by an emergency in the school."

Just as Daniels was finishing his explanation, Simpson walked in with a solemn face.

"Are there any further questions?" Barber asked. "Well, in that case, I will turn the meeting over to Mr. Simpson."

"Good morning, teachers. I'm sure, by now, that all of you are aware of the scheduled walkout by our student body this afternoon. I think we all must realize that our students at times act rashly and make threats which, in my experience, are never carried out. But if the students do attempt to walk out it will be your job as their teachers to continue with your ongoing educational program and be sure that the students are warned of the consequences of such actions."

"What are the consequences, Mr. Simpson?" yelled Feinberg.

"If a student does walk out," Simpson continued, "you should put down his name and get in touch with his parents. It would help matters if you teachers discouraged the students as much as possible from such rash actions."

Feinberg was on his feet now.

"Mr. Simpson, I hope you're not suggesting that we teachers try to stop these kids when they decide to leave this place. You know as well as I that if these kids decide to leave and we try to stop them we are going to be like Poland when the Nazis marched through."

"No, Mr. Feinberg," replied Simpson. "I don't expect

any teacher to physically restrain our students. But I do expect them to carry on with their programs even if there is only one student in the room. Are there any further questions concerning walkout procedure?"

No one raised a hand. Simpson looked relieved that he didn't have to answer any questions.

"Teachers, before you return to your rooms, I would suggest that we all re-evaluate our educational programs and specifically the motivating qualities of our bulletin boards. All too often we forget that students need an educational environment which all too often is missing at Du Sable. I think we all should try harder to construct a total learning environment at our school. Thank you for giving up your free time for the meeting."

Simpson quickly walked out of the room with the same solemn face he had entered with.

I got up and walked out with Portelli and Feinberg.

"Boy," I said, "Simpson sure looked pitiful up there. I almost felt sorry for him."

"That bastard doesn't deserve any pity," said Feinberg. "All year he's been hiding in that office while we've been getting our asses kicked. Not once has he said that the teachers have been doing a good job or lifted a finger to help us out with some of these goddam criminals in our classrooms. When some kid stabs Lincoln or threatens to walk out on you, all Simpson does is tell you that maybe your bulletin board isn't motivating, or call the kid's mother. Shit, man, if he had moved his ass out of that office and saw what was going on in the hallways and classrooms, maybe this ditto wouldn't be so much of a surprise. I told everyone from the beginning of the year that if you let these bastards get away with cursing you out, hitting you, stabbing you, cutting your classes, the next step is something like this. Simpson deserves everything those bastards can give him."

That afternoon I found myself, along with Portelli, in rather a bad strategic position if a walkout did occur. Since the beginning of the year both of us had been stationed on the first floor near the exit door to "actively supervise the hall." If the walkout took place according to schedule, Portelli and I would be the only obstacles between the kids and the exit. What worried me more when I showed up at my post was the absence of Portelli, who usually was sitting at a desk outside the office. That meant I was the only authority between the kids and the exit. I knew damn well that Simpson wasn't coming out of his office if the walkout came off, even though it would be a perfect opportunity to see how the kids reacted to the hallway bulletin boards. I was relieved to see Portelli come down the stairs with a lighted cigarette still in his mouth.

"Hey, Portelli," I yelled, "you better get that cigarette out of your mouth before Simpson catches you."

"Fuck him. Every man has a right to a last cigarette before he's executed."

We both laughed in a restrained manner, because it was almost time for our students to conduct their demonstration, as Simpson might put it.

"Portelli, do you think this thing is coming off?"

"Shit, who knows what these bastards will do? They're just not predictable. You know that. If someone has the balls to start it, then I think we've got trouble."

Mr. Jordan, the Master Teacher, came out in the hallway and looked up and down the corridor. He walked over to us near the gym lockers. I was sitting on top of a desk and Portelli was sitting behind it.

"Well, brothers," Jordan said, looking at his watch, "everything looks quiet, and its past two-thirty."

Both of us nodded in agreement, and I began to feel at ease. Jordan started back to the office when a doorway down the hall flew open and a student walked out of the room yelling at the top of his lungs, "Walkout, brothers—let's walk out," with his clenched fists raised in the air.

"Shit, Jones, we're in for it now. Listen, don't play John Wayne."

Jordan came running over to us and told us that if any more kids came out of the room not to let them go to their lockers. By now the doors to all the classrooms were flying open, banging against the corridor walls and making a terrible noise. Kids were all over the place, yelling "Walkout, walkout."

Jordan walked across the hall and started yelling at kids to return to their classrooms. He put himself up against one row of lockers and spread his arms out to prevent the kids from getting into their lockers.

"Come on, Portelli, we've got to help him."

"Jones, you're fuckin' crazy. He's black and you're white and you know who they'll kick the shit out of."

Where the hell was Simpson? The kids were pounding on classroom doors that hadn't opened and began to chant, "Walkout, walkout, walkout." Students were yelling at Jordan to get away from their lockers or they would "fuck him up." When he wouldn't budge, they just pried open the locker doors, with Jordan's extended arms bending in all directions. To my relief he finally gave up and walked back to the office, shaking his head.

Portelli had unlocked the exit door and the kids were beginning to funnel out. Two of my students, wearing red armbands with the initials CSDS on them (for Concerned Students of Du Sable), handed me a circular like the one I had received in my mailbox that morning.

"Say, Jones," said one kid, "we wants some action and we wants to be helped by you. Will ya?"

"Yes, John," I replied, "I'll talk to you about these demands."

"Man, we don't want no more of this talk bullshit. Talking's for fools. I ain't no fool."

"Thanks, John, for the circular."

"That's okay, Jones."

The screaming and yelling had stopped, and there were only a few kids left in the hallway. Most of the teachers were now standing outside of their classrooms just looking at each other.

I decided to go to my room and get my coat and briefcase. As I walked upstairs the emergency bell that Barber had talked about that morning began to ring.

When I arrived at my room there was glass all over the corridor from a broken door window in the classroom across from mine. Probably the glass broke when the kids swung the door open. My room was a mess when I walked in. Half the desks were turned over and there were paper airplanes everywhere. Some students had written "Power to the people" on my blackboard, and under it was written "Shorty and Charlie." At my desk sat a substitute teacher with long hair and a tie designed after the American flag. He looked like he needed a little cheering up. After I had gotten my coat out of the closet, I went over to my desk to get my briefcase.

"Pretty rough day," I said to the new teacher, as I bent under the desk for my briefcase.

"The roughest I've had ever since I started substituting," he replied. "Tell me," he continued, "have any of your students ever rolled up your pants while you were teaching them?"

I almost started to laugh, then I realized he was dead serious.

"You mean one of these kids tried to roll up your pants?" I asked.

"Man, not only did they try to roll up my pants, they *did* roll up my pants."

"Why the hell did you let them do that to you?"

"Well, I thought it would show them I wasn't prejudiced, that I was their friend."

"Listen," I said, "the only thing you showed those kids by letting them roll up your pants was that you're a damn fool. You're lucky they stopped with your pants. I'll talk to them tomorrow about what they did to you."

"Thank you," he replied. "Would you also ask them to return a gold pen I loaned out?"

"Yes, I'll ask them, but I can't guarantee anything."

On my way out the exit door I met one of my students from my morning language arts class.

"Here is my homework, Mr. Jones. I figure no one

going to come tomorrow so I wanted to give you this."

I had asked my morning classes to write a composition on what they thought about the planned walkout. They were free to write anything they wanted about either the validity of the demands or the rightness or wrongness of such a demonstration. Shirley, the girl who handed me the paper, was one of my best students and always handed in her work on time.

"Thank you, Shirley, for being so prompt. I will mark this tonight."

"Mr. Jones, it ain't no composition like you wanted, but some poetry. Is that all right?"

"Of course, Shirley. I told you that you could write what you wanted."

"See ya tomorrow, Mr. Jones, if they have school."

"Okay, Shirley."

While walking across the parking lot to sign out, I read Shirley's poem.

WALK OUT
by Shirley Baker

Walk out! Walk out! That's what it's all about.
People walking in and people walking out.
I doubt if they ever go back to school, 'cause a
  walkout person is nothing but a fool.
How are they going to get a good education by
  walking out?
But when they find out that walking out is just
  holding them back, they're going to pout.

16.
Conspiracy

When I arrived at school the next morning and looked at the faculty bulletin board, I was not surprised to find a notice for all staff members to report to Room 179 at 8:24 A.M. for a meeting. Simpson had to do something, even if it was only to call us together and bitch about our lesson plans or bulletin boards. At least he would be covering himself with the people downtown, who probably were already viewing the walkout episode as a "black eye" on his record.

What did surprise me was a memo in my mailbox instructing all concerned black teachers to report to Room 179 after lunch to discuss the walkout. I couldn't figure out why the memo was in my mailbox unless, of course, my last name had caused the mistake. It was, after all, a "slave name."

As I walked up the stairs to Room 179 I began to collect my thoughts about the demands of the students and the actions they had already taken. Along with my students, I was fed up with the school facilities, the hoodlums who roamed the halls, and Simpson's pedantry. But I also felt that even if all the demands of the concerned students were met, they would still be getting an inferior education.

It seemed to me that everyone—from my students to the black militants—had missed the point. Years of discrimination had created in the ghetto surrounding Du Sable an environment that was anathema to education. My students were so far behind that no program could possibly overcome the academic deficiencies caused by fourteen or fifteen years of ghetto life.

The students of Du Sable needed more than black teachers, a black principal, or a new lunch room. They needed to be able to walk to school without being hassled by gangs. They needed a stable home life where a father had a job that paid good wages. They needed housing built for humans, not animals, and, most important, they needed to believe that what they learned at Du Sable would make a difference in their life. To meet these needs would mean the total restructuring of priorities within our society. Because I believed this was too much to ask of our political leaders at this time, I guess I could understand the race hatred in Du Sable.

What bothered me most about my conclusions was the total disavowal of my college idealism. I was left with only a crippling cynicism to deal with my students and my colleagues. So many things had gone wrong in my eight months at Du Sable that I began to think there was a conspiracy against me, the faculty, the kids, and anybody or anything that tried to do something in an inner-city school. I was mad that on our faculty we had good people, black and white, who cared and were being used by the kids, Simpson, and the Board. These teachers who cared were the ones who were getting hurt, either physically or mentally. Too many good people's efforts were being wasted by too many omnipotent administrators, who would ultimately blame these same people when trouble came. That's how it was. Everyone was trying to cover himself. Unless someone, somewhere in power was willing to stand up and admit that something was terribly wrong with a system, whether school or governmental, that could not educate its young to function in an advanced industrial society, then that system would continue merrily on its way, using adults as well as children as pawns in a losing game.

My thoughts were interrupted by Portelli, who was waving a piece of paper in front of my face, yelling at me to read it. The paper was another ditto which read:

ATTENTION

The administration of Du Sable Upper Grade Center has made the decision on who should fill the Master Teacher vacancy. His qualifications are:

1. White
2. Two years' experience
3. Draft dodger
4. Student at Kent Law School

The concerned students of Du Sable Upper Grade Center feel this man is unqualified to become our new Master Teacher. We feel there are black teachers with more experience and education who should receive this promotion.

After reading the dittoed message I turned to Portelli, who was visibly upset.

"Where did you get this, Portelli?"

"The goddam bastards are handing these things out in front of the school."

"Portelli, how in hell did they get this personal information about Mr. Shapiro?"

"Who the hell knows, Jones. Shit. Simpson's so

fuckin' scared of these kids that he probably let them walk into his office and look at his personnel files."

I was about to ask Feinberg what he thought about the new circular when Simpson walked in with Barber.

"Good morning, teachers," Simpson began, a big smile on his face. "I thought we would use the free time available to us today to conduct workshops in our respective subject areas. Hopefully, some new ideas will emerge from these meetings which will help us deal more successfully with our student body."

Simpson was unbelievable! His entire student body had walked out on him, somebody was going through our personnel files, and the black teachers were holding a meeting that afternoon—and Simpson's only response was to conduct workshops. Feinberg was right. Anything these kids did to him, he deserved. I raised my hand.

"Mr. Simpson," I began. "Aren't we even going to discuss what happened yesterday?"

"Mr. Jones," Simpson replied, "I am quite aware of what happened. But I thought that rather than just sit around here and discuss the walkout, we would better spend our time in workshops developing innovative programs for our students when they return."

"Mr. Simpson," yelled Feinberg, "I think what Mr. Jones is trying to say is that no workshops or innovative ideas are going to solve the problems that made our student body walk out."

"I must disagree with you, Mr. Feinberg," replied Simpson. "It has been my experience . . ."

A teacher named Faulkner jumped up from his seat and cut Simpson off in the middle of his sentence.

"Mr. Simpson, the teachers are sick of workshops,

bulletin boards, and plan books. They ain't going to do shit, and I think we better get talking about what's really wrong with this school before you lose your faculty."

Everyone in the room let out a cheer and began to clap. Simpson just stood there with his eyes almost coming out of his head. I felt a little sorry for him because nothing in this school went by the textbook, and Simpson certainly was not known for his originality.

"Are Mr. Faulkner's feelings," Simpson mumbled in a low voice, "the consensus of opinion in this room?"

Everyone raised his hand. Clips stood up in the back of the room and asked for recognition. Simpson just waved his hand for Clips to speak.

"Mr. Simpson, I think I can speak for the entire staff when I say that we are not mad at you for what has happened, nor do we question your ability. We still recognize you as our principal. What the staff is asking is that some soul-searching be done by both administration and staff into the crisis that confronts our school. We must come together and find solutions to make Du Sable a good school and one . . ."

"Mr. Simpson," cut in Feinberg, "I think we ought to get down to the issues immediately and see where we are and where we are going. But first, Mr. Simpson, I would like to know if you are aware of the fact that some of our students are publicizing private information on individual faculty members. I was under the impression that the personnel forms we filed at the beginning of the year were private, and that all information on that form had to have our prior consent before it was divulged to anyone."

Simpson stepped forward with a big grin on his face and leaned on the desk in front of him.

"Yes, Mr. Feinberg, I am aware that personnel information has leaked out to our students. This unfortunate breach of privacy has occurred because my personnel files are gone."

I didn't know whether to laugh or cry.

"Yes, I'm sorry to admit that my personnel files are gone."

"Where the hell are they?" yelled Feinberg.

"I don't know, Mr. Feinberg. I walked into my office this morning and found the entire file drawer gone."

Some of the faculty members began to laugh. Even Simpson had a silly grin on his face. Feinberg just stood at his desk with his mouth open. Portelli leaned over to me and pulled my arm.

"Jesus Christ, Jones, I'm surprised Simpson showed up with his pants on."

"Mr. Simpson, may I have the floor?" asked Miss Smith, our music teacher.

Simpson didn't say a word but again just motioned her to begin.

"I have been discussing this walkout with several teachers, and we came to the conclusion that what our students are asking for is valid and that we teachers should join our students by walking out, too."

Simpson looked like he needed cold water splashed on his face.

Lincoln was now on his feet, yelling at Miss Smith from across the room. "Miss Smith, I disagree on your course of action. Could you please tell me what is valid about our students' demands?"

"Why, Mr. Lincoln, I am surprised that you don't

162

agree. Brother, just take a look at this school. All the windows are broken. Plaster is falling off the walls, our kids got no gym. What could be more valid than asking for better facilities?"

Everyone's eyes shifted to Lincoln, who remained seated while Miss Smith was cataloguing the woes of Du Sable. When she finished, he sat there and just looked around the room. He stood up slowly and faced Miss Smith, who was seated in the back of the room, and began to talk in a low, distinct voice.

"When I was in Boston, there was a school there named Harvard. Now this school had some pretty old buildings and yet they managed to do some teaching."

The entire faculty burst out laughing. Even Simpson, in his depressed state, managed to get a smile out. Portelli leaned over and shook my leg.

"Goddam it, Jones, why are you laughing? He's right."

Before the laughter had died down, Hicks, our white radical in residence, was on his feet yelling for quiet.

"I think we teachers should follow Miss Smith's suggestion and walk out as a symbolic gesture. Maybe the publicity will bring some reforms to the school."

"Bullshit," Feinberg yelled. "If we walk out of here the Board of Education will have this school fully staffed within a week, and we'll be on the street looking like fools."

Hicks and Benjamin, another white radical, stood up and began to yell, "Let's walk out." The shouting back and forth ended when Mrs. Harris, our Master Teacher, stood up and Simpson recognized her.

Mrs. Harris had been at Du Sable for only three days but had managed in that brief span of time to build a reputation as a militant by telling several white teachers that they were "castrating little black children" in their classrooms.

"Mr. Simpson, I think that the white teachers in this school are involved in a conspiracy to castrate little black children and deprive them of their education. Mr. Hicks's enthusiasm for walking out verifies my contention."

Coach Mills burst out laughing in the back of the room. Some teachers, both white and black, started yelling at Mrs. Harris to sit down. Simpson, who was now seated on the desk in front of the room, looked overwhelmed. Teachers began to walk out of the meeting. I was so disgusted with Du Sable that I just wanted to walk out the front door and never return.

I started to do just that when Portelli caught me on the steps leading down to the first floor.

"What the hell is wrong, Jones? You really look depressed."

"What's wrong with you, Portelli, didn't you hear what that black bitch said?"

"Hell yes, didn't you hear the Coach and I laughing in the back of the room?"

"How can you laugh at something like that, Portelli?"

"Jones, this is your first year and I understand how you feel. Take my advice and forget about what she said, and just remember there are only two months left till we graduate these bastards."

"Hell, Portelli, doesn't it bother you that none of the kids you're graduating can read, and that bitch blames you for it?"

"It bothered me last year, but not this year."

"What happened to you in that year, Portelli?"

"Jones, after a year you learn that there's no place for white people in schools like this. After you admit that, then you just sit and listen to these fools make their accusations while you pick up your check and look for another job."

"But, Portelli, I'm a good teacher, and I could do something with these kids if I had a chance."

"Jones, face the fact that you aren't getting a chance. And that's that."

I just stood there staring at Portelli.

"Listen, Jones," Portelli began to smile, "why don't you take Mr. Lincoln's advice and go to Boston and find those old buildings where they do some teaching?"

"You're nuts, Portelli. There isn't a chance they would let me teach at Harvard."

"Jones, you have more of a chance teaching at Harvard than you do here. And that's what you learn in a year."

17.
"What Does it Matter?"

*A*s I walked across the parking lot to the high school auditorium where my class was practicing for their graduation, I felt a sense of accomplishment. I had made it, as Portelli would put it. To many teachers, just "making it" through an entire year is hardly enough. But to most of the inner-city teachers I knew, making it was the only thing that counted after a while. It kept you going. When the end finally arrived and you found yourself in one piece physically and mentally, it was a triumphant moment in your teaching career.

My class was already at the auditorium, but I had to find the stragglers and get them seated in their proper rows. I hoped that my last contact with Du Sable would be as uneventful as possible, with everything coming off according to plan. Maybe a successful graduation practice would leave me with some hope for these kids and the school.

Clips and Miss Smith were on the stage giving orders through a microphone to individual teachers who had either lost their classes or were trying to hide from them. Because of his many years of service at Du Sable, Clips organized the yearly graduation ceremonies. Miss Smith was the school's music teacher; it was her job to get all the kids who were graduating to stop singing songs by the Supremes and learn the prescribed songs voted on by a coterie of experienced teachers, led by Clips.

I was prepared for a long rehearsal because Clips was not known for his brevity. For him, the graduation ceremony was the culmination of eight years of work by "our students," and therefore it had to be directed in the tradition of Cecil B. DeMille. As I sat down in my assigned seat in back and watched Portelli's class enter with Cassandra Fulton yelling at the top of her lungs, "I ain't going up on that stage," I began to wonder if parting the Red Sea would be as difficult as getting Cassandra up on that stage.

"May I have your attention? May I have your attention?" began Clips. You could barely hear what he was saying because of all the noise in the auditorium. He bent over and made some adjustments on a speaker next to him and began again.

"May I have your attention, please?"

Some of the kids in the front of the auditorium began to sit down and pay attention to Clips, but generally the entire place was up for grabs. Miss Smith grabbed the microphone away from Clips and began to scream:

"Brothers and sisters, let's get quiet. Come on, brothers and sisters, let's show some pride."

The appeal to pride didn't work either. Kids were still running up and down the aisles, hitting each other, and throwing all kinds of food. The place began to smell like a movie theater. Miss Smith bent down and turned on what must have been a record player because you could hear music come through the speakers. But I couldn't quite make out what she was playing.

Clips now grabbed the microphone from Miss Smith

168

and began asking for attention again. I stood up and went over to my class to try to settle them down. Some extra teachers began to arrive and to patrol the aisles, showing students which section they should be in and physically putting recalcitrant students in their seats.

Order was finally achieved by the brief appearance of Coach Mills and his baseball bat. He walked up and down the aisles yelling at the top of his lungs, "I want all black ass in their seats," swinging his baseball bat indiscriminately. When the Coach disappeared, it was up to us to hold the line.

"Now that I have your attention," Clips yelled through the microphone, "I would like to take this opportunity to tell you how wonderful it is to see all of you here at such an important time in your life. I want to compliment you on how you entered this auditorium and your deportment thus far."

I was as shocked at Clips's opening statement as was Feinberg, who was standing by the stage looking up at Clips with his mouth wide open, just as he had done when Simpson told him the personnel files were missing. Maybe the stage lights were impairing Clips's vision. What a time for him to go soft. Oh, if only the Coach had stayed.

"Now that we are all settled," Clips continued, "I will tell you what we are going to do this afternoon. First, we are all going to stand and sing the graduation theme song. Then, we are going to practice . . ."

"Fuck you, Clips," someone yelled from a hallway door at the back of the auditorium, cutting Clips off in the middle of his sentence.

This was not unexpected. When the Upper Grade

Center used the high school auditorium, some high school student would inevitably yell profanities through the hallway door on the balcony at whomever was on the stage. I felt sorry for Clips because he took things like this personally. After he finished scanning the balcony, he began again.

"When we finish singing our theme song . . ."

"Get fucked, man."

". . . then we will practice marching," Clips shouted angrily into the microphone.

"Why don't you march, old man?"

Several teachers ran up the balcony steps to the hallway doors, but I knew they wouldn't catch anyone. The best way to handle those hoodlums in the hallway was just to ignore them. It seemed that the more you ran after them or the more you yelled at them, the more they enjoyed annoying you. The only person in the school who could handle them was the Coach, who attributed his success to "dealing with the black bastards on their level," which to the Coach meant "beating their black ass until they can't stand no more."

"Members of the graduating class," Clips continued, "let's not have this graduation disrupted by outsiders. Remember this is *your* graduation. Only you can make it a meaningful experience. Let's all stand and sing loudly the graduation theme song, 'Dream the Impossible Dream.' "

I almost burst out laughing. What a perfect song for this production! Clips had to be admired for his innocent idealism. He never gave up trying to prove that Du Sable was Disneyland, not the Black Hole of Calcutta.

After everyone was standing, Miss Smith began to sing "The Impossible Dream." Since the school had run out of ditto paper, and had few ditto machines that worked anyway, there was a limited supply of song sheets for the students to use. So, except for Miss Smith and a few classes in the front of the room, most of the kids in the auditorium were just standing in place, talking with their neighbors or spitting sunflower seeds at each other, dropping foreign objects down girls' blouses, or just looking up at the ceiling while sucking on a dill pickle.

Clips grabbed the microphone away from Miss Smith, and as if he were at a rock festival, began to yell, "Let's all sing together, 'Dream the Impossible Dream.'"

Although no one responded to Clips's efforts at charismatic appeal, he did have a good baritone. Paper planes began to fly across the auditorium and a loud, verbal fight broke out between two girls in the front. But Clips and Miss Smith kept on singing. They were determined to finish, no matter what happened.

Some high school kids got together in the back of the auditorium and yelled, "Fuck you," in unison, just as Clips and Miss Smith finished their song.

Clips stepped way from Miss Smith and began to grin as he spoke.

"I want to compliment all of you on the way you performed that song. I am proud of all of you. Let's all clap for our performance."

Kids began clapping, whistling, banging their shoes on the backs of chairs. Clips was making a fool out of himself. How long would he continue this masquerade? Why didn't he just send everyone back to their rooms to settle down? Better yet, why didn't

Simpson just call the whole thing off? I had only one day left, and I began to feel my luck running out.

"Teachers," Clips began yelling over the clapping, "please take your students up to the balcony and we will practice marching into the auditorium. Can you hear me back there? Take your classes to the balcony."

The teachers near the front began to move their kids out as well as they could. I went over to my class and started shouting directions at them. Most of them just looked up at me and smiled while continuing to eat their dill pickles. They were as confused as I was. Finally, in desperation, I began lifting kids bodily out of their seats and directing them to the balcony entrance. After a couple of minutes all of them got the general idea and were moving out. Two or three of my students had vanished completely, but then, that was nothing unusual.

When I reached the balcony stairwell there was a fight in progress between a girl and a boy in Portelli's class. Clips and Miss Smith were yelling at Portelli and me to break it up and get the kids moving. I almost turned around to scream at both of them when I saw Portelli jump on the boy.

I reached over and grabbed the girl by the arm. Her elbow hit me in the eye, knocking my glasses off. I bent down and picked up my glasses and sat in a seat, dabbing my eye with a handkerchief. Portelli came over to me and asked me how I was.

"I'm okay, Portelli."

"Look what that bastard did to me, Jones." Portelli rolled up his pants leg revealing a gash on his leg.

"How did he do that, Portelli?"

"The son of a bitch kicked me."

When I leaned my head back in an attempt to relieve the pain in my eye and head, I noticed a plaque above the stage which read: "PEACE IF POSSIBLE: BUT JUSTICE AT ANY RATE."

That did it. Something in me snapped. The only way I was going to get justice in this school was to get the hell out of Du Sable and never come back. I got up and walked to the front exit doors. Clips and Miss Smith were yelling something at me, but I just kept going.

When I reached the parking lot exit door, I opened it and took a big breath of air. It was all over for me. No more orders. No more insults. No more gangbangers. No more bulletin boards. No Simpson. No more militants. No more community. And no more kids.

Just before I reached the other side of the faculty parking lot, I saw Simpson's car with its rear window totally smashed out. There was glass all over the place. He would probably blame our bulletin boards for his broken windows. After all, if the kids were motivated they wouldn't be in the parking lot breaking windows. The bastard deserved everything he got.

I went to my room for my briefcase and then went to the office to sign out. There was a big sign on the faculty bulletin board above the time sheets, which read:

TEACHERS ! ! !

Please ride your bicycles to school tomorrow.

R. Simpson

Simpson was standing in back of the sign with a big grin on his face, watching me sign out.

"Mr. Jones, is the graduation practice over yet?" he asked.

173

"It is for me, Mr. Simpson," I replied. "What's the sign for, Mr. Simpson?"

"Well, Mr. Jones, every year some of our students threaten to damage the teachers' cars on the last day of school. After what happened to my car today, I thought it best to take some precautions."

I was glad this was my last day. How could you be expected to teach in a school where a principal put up a sign telling you to ride a bike to school and could keep smiling after some gangbangers just busted up his car?

I signed out, said goodbye to Simpson, and hurriedly walked out of the building. Halfway down the front steps some kid called to me.

"Say, Jack, you a Mr. Jones?"

I turned around to find a boy about fifteen or sixteen wearing an undershirt with no sleeves, a chain around his neck with a bullet on it, an earring in his left ear, and a big, black leather cap on his head.

"Yeah, I'm Mr. Jones."

"Hey, man, why'd you fail me?"

"I don't even know you," I replied.

"What does that matter, Jones?"

I just stared at the grin on his face. I had seen this kid once at the beginning of the year, and he was asking me why I hadn't passed him.

"Well, Jones, why'd you fail me?"

I turned away from him and walked around the building to the bus stop. After boarding the bus and taking a seat in the back, I stared out the window at the pawnshops, honky-tonks, record shops, barbecue joints, and bars that were part of the ghetto neighborhood. As the bus started up I wondered what it all did matter.

174

Postscript

After rereading *Students: Do Not Push Your Teacher Down the Stairs on Friday*, I am afraid that many readers will think it is just another funny book about incompetent school administrators, or, even worse, a subtle diatribe against black people in America. Neither of these estimates touches the issue I was trying to come to grips with—that of racism. Both are understandable, however, because they offer an easy way out for a society that is bored or angry with problems that "don't go away." If the book can be labeled either "funny" or "racist," it can be ignored or enjoyed, depending on who reads it; the causes and consequences of a school like Du Sable need not be considered.

Unless Americans recognize Du Sable for what it is— a human tragedy which is indigenous to the places where blacks live, and not merely an aberration of post-industrial society—America faces the prospect of two societies: one black and one white, one poor and one well-off, one unemployed and one employed, one trying to tear down and one trying to support the country, and one hating while the other hates back. No society can survive under such conditions.

Historically, people (not only Americans) have always ignored social injustice when it has involved a

change of attitudes. It is easier to pay higher taxes for a
war on poverty than to let a black man move in next
door; or to read about conditions in the ghetto on the
commuter train that travels through on its way to
the suburbs, than to let your child be bused to an
integrated school. Efforts to understand one's racism or
to try to do something about it are painful. They fall
on those most incapable of handling it—the "silent
majority."

But, unlike other times, there is no longer any place
to hide. Poverty programs have failed. Schools have
failed. Police have failed. The national guard has
failed. Prisons have failed. Black capitalism has failed.
Nothing works anymore, and sometimes a Hitlerite
formula (the South Dakota solution) sounds attractive.

The question of race in our society has resolved
itself into one of attitudes and feelings. Do I accept a
black man as an equal, or do I continue treating him
like a subhuman, thus demeaning myself and that
nation which announced to the world that "all men are
created equal"?

To be sure, the question of race in America is far
more complicated than I have briefly suggested. I do not
expect attitudes to change overnight—or, for that
matter, at all in the coming decades. What I do hope is
that people will realize the social costs involved in
perpetuating a racist society. It is not pleasant to walk
the street at night fearing for your life, or to send your
child to school not knowing whether he will return,
or to pay exorbitant taxes for jails and police that don't
protect, or to pay for a welfare system that perpetuates
poverty, or to work next to a man who hates you
because of the color of your skin—black or white.

These are the tangible social costs of ghetto neighborhoods, inadequate schools, and substandard employment for blacks. Unless this vicious circle is broken, we must all fall victim to Sophocles' observation, "Evil seems good to him who is doomed to suffer."